TRUE: From the Inside Out

By: Danielle Martin

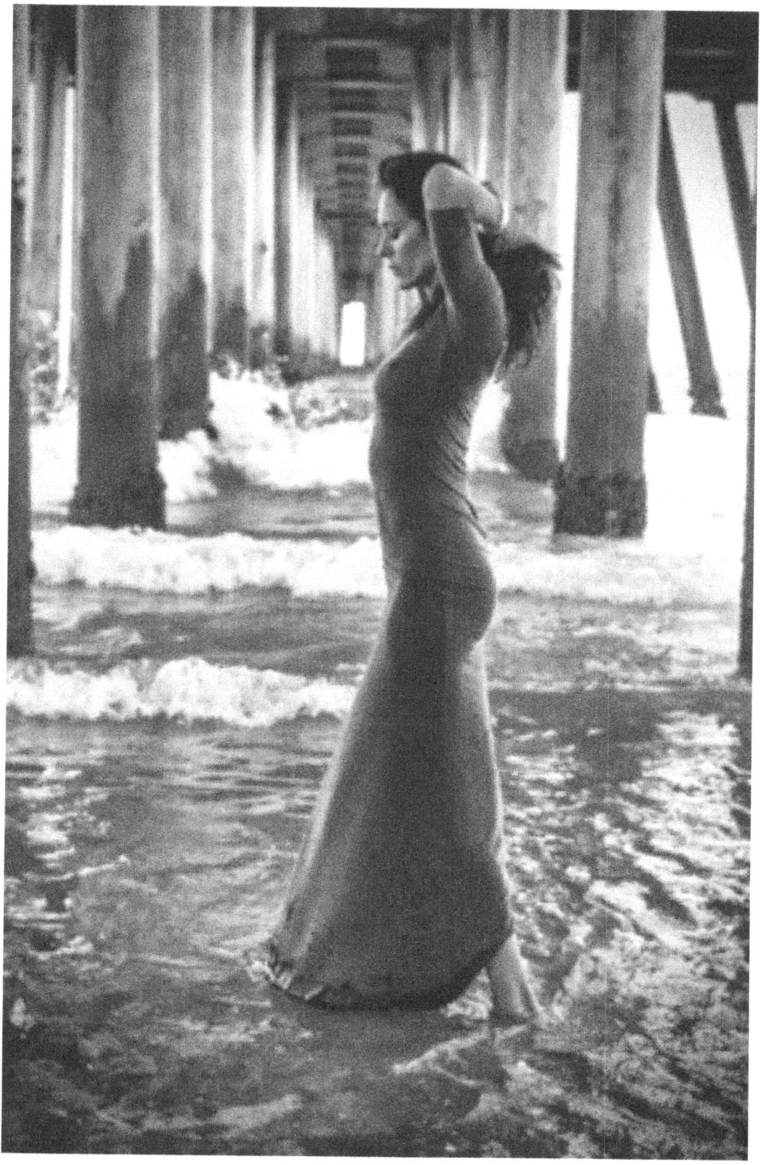

DEDICATION

I'd like to dedicate this book to my Grandpa Sam. There isn't a day that goes by you aren't in my heart or in my thoughts. Thank you for inspiring me and for your influence and unconditional love while you were here.

To John C, thank you for always protecting me and for loving me like a daughter.

To my boys, Bryce and Brody…may you always remember how much I love you and how important it always will be to love yourselves.

FOREWORD

It takes an awful lot for someone to get my attention as either an athlete or entrepreneur. This is because most of my clients are internationally known celebrities, athletes, or top 1% entrepreneurs. Many of them have gone on to follow in my footsteps by earning world titles or recognition in the Hall of Fame. However, from my first encounter with Danielle Martin, she had my attention and respect not only as an athlete and entrepreneur but as a humble and inspiring human.

I have coached Martial artists for more than 40 years and entrepreneurs for more than 20 years. It has been my experience that many people either have the strength and stamina to pursue their art form or the smarts and savviness to formulate and fulfill a meaningful business mission. Danielle has impressed me with her unwavering commitment to and passion for both. In addition to being a world class athlete, Danielle is driven by what I call Purpose Driven Prosperity, meaning that her quest for business success is fueled by her motivation to help others.

She is determined to empower others while continually evolving, growing and improving herself as a person and entrepreneur at the same time.

What Danielle has accomplished in her lifetime thus far is very impressive by any standard. But what makes her so compelling to me is what she has had to overcome in order to be the successful athlete, mom, role model and mentor she is today. This book offers a personal glimpse into Danielle's journey through the years as she has traveled from tears of sadness to tears of gladness. From being beaten down to building others up. Danielle is proof positive that even when challenges abound, personal success and happiness can be an active choice. Her experiences reinforce the notion that other people only have as much physical, mental and emotional power over us as we choose to allow them to have. And especially that some boundaries are truly needed while others need to be eliminated altogether.

It's an honor to call Danielle Martin a friend, client and partner. Her passion for helping others is second to none. I hope that what Danielle shares in this book will inspire you to also live your life to your fullest potential while committing to help others do the same in the process.

Dr. Reggie Cochran, PhD, DCH, CPMA

www.facebook.com/officialreggiecochran

www.reggiecochran.com

INTRODUCTION

*"Though nothing can bring back the hour of splendor in
the grass, of glory in the flower,
We will grieve not, rather find
Strength in what remains behind."*

--William Wordsworth

There are times that everyone grapples with the fragility of life as we confront our frailties, weaknesses, fears, and failures. Accepting our imperfections but having the strength and insight to learn from our mistakes and then share these with others is a uniquely human trait that sets us apart from every other creature on this planet. I wrote this book at a time in my life when I was struggling to understand myself, come to terms with my own past and present, and in hopes of candidly and honestly embracing my true self. I had hopes of taking charge of my future health and happiness. In the process, I refused to be defined by injustice, weaknesses, or losses that I experienced, but to at least be honest in recognizing these so that I could ultimately move beyond them. I know that in many instances when we look back on life, we can never right the wrongs. However, I can write the wrongs. And in doing so in these pages, I have tried to look with candor at my own self as well as the people and situations that have been critical in shaping me into the person that I am today. We thrive or fail not only by the grace of our own strength and sense but also in reflection of the individuals and experiences that collectively shape us on our life journey.

I feel I have lived a relatively extreme life marked by many highs and lows and I have been both incredibly challenged and yet incredibly blessed. I can't change anything in my past, but I have always tried to take charge of my own future by finding strength in any form or fashion available. In writing this book, I have tried to look back and take away a meaningful lesson from every heartbreak, loss, mistake, or failure. I will *grieve not, rather find strength in what remains behind...*

I made the decision to share my life story in these pages in hope of inspiring others to be brave in understanding, confronting, challenging, and ultimately loving and accepting their own true selves. I think there are a lot of people out there who have stories to tell and they don't do it because they are waiting for some kind of permission or greater reason to just sit down and do it. Well here I am, sitting down and just doing it. Writing a book, pouring my heart onto pages for all to see. I have to say upfront that I'm not an author. I didn't take classes on how to write a book. I am sitting here now and typing whatever comes to mind and all that is waiting to be seen and heard. I guess what I'm saying is that if I can do this, anyone can. You don't need permission from anyone, just do it.

People often mistake strength with ego and weakness with heart. I believe it's actually the opposite. It takes great strength to truly love yourself as well as to love others. Ego is a blinder to life, to love, and to any kind of growth or evolvement. It doesn't matter what you do for a living or who you "think" you are, how above others you "think" you are, if you're not a good person on the inside, you are nothing more than ego. Don't judge a man's position, judge the man. I look back on everything I've done in my life, the things I've been attracted to as a person, the sports and activities I've engaged in, and the kind of people I have surrounded myself with. The way life shapes and seemingly prepares us for what is to come in the future is fascinating and I feel as if we all unfold like a little love story even in spite of our darkest times.

    I spend a lot of time working with children, teens, young adults, and even corporations and I try to teach the importance of recognizing and capitalizing on individual strengths and the value of unwavering strength in the face of adversity. I sometimes feel my message is undermined by the perception that my life has been blessed and golden, and that I don't really know what it means to suffer or struggle. By sharing a candid account of my life, I hope that anyone who looks to me for answers will know and believe that I too have been alone, I have been scared, and I have questioned whether my life had any purpose or meaning whatsoever. As unique as the specific details of my life are to me, I recognize that the broader issues of love and trust, faith and friendship, hope and despair, sickness and health, and even neglect and evil intentions are universal. These may manifest in different ways for different people, but they are undeniably some of the commonalities in the human experience. These are the things that make us human, that can bond us together and even tear us apart. And so, this book is about my journey in finding strength through adversity. It's about character, integrity, courage, friendship, love, acceptance, and the power of a positive attitude. These pages reflect my heart, my history, my hopes, and my True Me: From the Inside Out.

Chapter One

"ADULT IN A CHILD'S BODY"

"If only she could be so oblivious again, to feel such love without knowing it,
mistaking it for laughter"
-Markus Zusak, The Book Thief

I have vivid memories of my earliest childhood years in Couer d'Alene, Idaho. I can distinctly recall the way our house was configured, how the furniture was arranged, and even the texture and smells of the couch and carpet. When I picture myself there, I immediately associate with the feelings of tension and stress that were all too familiar for the little girl in what should have been her safest haven. I look back now, and in my mind's eye I can truly see the child I was; I was that little girl in her home and I observe her body language as the turmoil swirls around her. No matter how many years have gone by, I can't help but reflect on this time in my life with a detached sense of sadness for the little girl that once was.

My parents were young when they had me, and I am sure my arrival was completely unexpected and not enthusiastically embraced. Nobody has ever said as much, but I feel pretty comfortable making that assumption! My mom and dad had frequent and intense battles with one another as far back as I can remember. I never got used to seeing them fight or to hearing the anger in their voices; I just couldn't understand how two people who loved each other enough to have me could treat each other so horribly. As unsettling as their confrontations were for me to witness, their battles were sometimes preferred over the wildly unpredictable elements of their partying lifestyle that took place in our home. Their moods and behaviors seemed to vacillate wildly between the two extremes of fighting and reckless partying. Accordingly, I woke up most days feeling tentative and uncertain as to what kind of day it would be and which side of my parents I should be prepared to handle. I couldn't have pinpointed what exactly was wrong, but I was intuitive enough to know that I craved something very different. I was incredibly independent and very guarded; no matter how insecure or threatened I felt, I would never let myself display any outward signs of sadness, fear, or emotion. I know enough now to recognize that

I likely formed early defense mechanisms in order to protect myself from the dangers I perceived all around me. I also can say that today my childhood home would be called "dysfunctional" because of the constant chaos and unhealthy situations for a growing child.

Although I always knew my family was unconventional, I can laugh now as I recognize some instances that believe was my true childish naiveté. I remember once when my mom was trying to be "normal," and she hosted a Tupperware party in our home. In an attempt to be helpful, I came into the living room and asked the ladies if anyone would like "a toke off the bong." It was then that I first learned that things that might be perfectly appropriate in certain social situations may be completely inappropriate in others! My parents grew pot plants in my bedroom under glowing pink heat lamps, and I never had a clue that this was both unusual and illegal; I even helped take care of "my" plants with pride. I became accustomed to the fact that my parents were always living fast and to the extreme. So, I didn't think it unusual if they left me at home alone during their nude water ski runs at midnight, invited friends and strangers alike into our home at all hours, or when they both snuck people into the house when the other was not around.

    I never really felt secure or safe with either of my parents, although I definitely favored my dad. Even with his temper, I loved him and always tried hard to earn his approval and love. I could be in my bedroom and would hear him start his dirt bike up and I would charge outside before he could leave without me. He would race through the woods with me sitting right up on the gas tank with my little hands tightly grasping the handlebars. He took me waterskiing on the lake and would thrash me on the inner tube that he dragged behind our boat. He was always playing catch with me and encouraging me to go bigger and bigger with everything I did. When my dad wasn't around, I would often be outside doing my best to get in on the t-ball games the neighborhood boys would play. In those early years, most of my happier memories were outdoors-- making forts, playing with animals, in the water, or with a ball in my hand. I am grateful to my dad for exposing me to all of those things that I loved both then and now, and for encouraging me from an early age to take risks and always be the best I could be. He pushed me and challenged me from an early age, and from that I learned to always push and challenge myself.

I never truly felt that my mom was totally available to me. Being available isn't just being in the same space physically and doing what needs to be done. It's a feeling that you get when a person is connected to you and attentive to your basic emotional needs in that shared space. I have always been sensitive to human and animal energies, and I sensed that my mom had something else on her mind or another agenda she would rather be focused on when she was with me. I never felt secure in her company. I know now that she was struggling with many things, including stress in her relationship with my dad, and with her addictions. Quite frankly, she was probably also just working on growing up herself and perhaps it's unfair to have expected her to be all that I needed at that time. I don't remember doing many things at all with my mom. I do remember that she was a professional at cooking out of boxes. We were raised on Hamburger Helper, Kraft Macaroni & Cheese, cut-up hot dogs with ketchup and canned green beans. My dad would shoot deer sometimes or he would fish for trout in the lake. I do remember my mom baking sometimes, but I wasn't allowed to eat her "special" homemade brownies because they were only for the adults and kept in high cabinets.

One day, when I was four years old, I got mad and told my mom I was going to run away to California. When she told me that it would be fine with her, I knew I had to stick to my guns and put action behind my words. I went straight outside, hopped into her car and shifted it into neutral gear. I remember the smell of her Mercedes and the olive-green color of her leather seats. She smoked in her car, so it had that unmistakable leather and cigarette smell combined with a hint of her perfume. The driveway was very steep, so the car instantly started to roll backward with me in the driver's seat. I am certain my mom must have nearly had a heart attack when she heard the gravel growling beneath the tires of her car. The car rolled pretty fast down the hill, crossed a street and crashed straight into a pine tree. My mom came running out of the house, yelling of course, and even crying. I was calm, still hanging onto the steering wheel, feeling quite proud of myself, and still in one piece. I was probably giving her an "I told you I would" kind of look with a hint of "sorry." Looking back, I was probably just trying to get her attention or punish her for her shortcomings as I saw them.

I absolutely had a survival instinct all along, but I am sure it was my sister Sadie's arrival when I was three years old that evoked my first protective instinct. I always perceived that there was a real need to look out for her. As a baby myself, there were few things that I could truly control, but Sadie's safety was always a priority for me and I tried to control that as best as I could. I was actually intrigued to later learn that researchers have recently discovered that instead of displaying the classic "fight or flight" response to danger or stress, females are actually more likely to "tend and befriend" in times of stress or crisis. This makes sense from an evolutionary standpoint, because a mother has never likely been able to flee to safety with young children or fight off whatever predator might be attacking her brood. Instead, soothing frightened children, nurturing, reassuring, protecting, and forming social alliances for future safety might be more effective strategies that seem to better characterize the female response in times of stress or danger. This concept of "tend and befriend" makes a lot of sense to me now and I see how that drive has personally governed many of the choices that I have made-for better and for worse- throughout my life.

It was an honor and a duty to watch over Sadie, even though my mom will tell you I tried on several occasions to get rid of her. She tells funny stories about my antics with her, my ideas, and my schemes. I can assure you that is all they were! As much as I didn't want Sadie copying me, touching me, or touching my things, I truly had her back and watched over her in situations that were inappropriate for either of us. However, that didn't stop me from giving Sadie her very first driving lesson when she was still a tiny thing- probably about two years of age. I put my sister in the same seat of the same car and showed her how to shift the car into neutral gear. I stepped away from the car after her private lesson and away she went, backward down the driveway and straight into the same pine tree. My sister also emerged unscathed, but this stunt with her had wrecked the car even worse than mine had the first time. I thought this was funny, of course, but my mom gave me a good beating and I believe I didn't do it again.

When my parents were wrapped up with their partying, it didn't leave much security or supervision for Sadie and me. Somehow, from a very young age, I would sense when it wasn't safe and would stay especially close to Sadie. I didn't like some of my dad's friends- and for sure the neighborhood boy who eventually cornered me and crossed some lines. Of course when you're young like that you don't have the words to describe your feelings or to explain the danger you are in. This boy told me that if I did find the words or courage to actually tell my parents, then he would kill them. I locked those experiences up in my mind and threw away the key, trying to protect my parents. I always just tried to compensate and survive.

I spent most of my free time at home in Idaho outside and alone. My parents liked to breed Labrador Retrievers, so there was always a trusted four-legged friend around for me to play with and explore with. I had a black lab I adored from about the time I turned one year old until he passed away when I was sixteen. I loved and felt connected with all animals and I was especially enamored with horses from the earliest time I can remember. I used to ask my dad for a horse more than I asked for anything else. I am grateful still today for the animals in my life, and feel there is always something to be learned from them if we open our hearts and listen.

I was five years old when my parents finally divorced. Sadie and I lived with my mom then, and I remember her having most of the responsibilities of caring for us at that point. She struggled to stay in one place for longer than a few months at a time. We moved a lot, and we ended up living for various lengths of time in Idaho, Lake Tahoe, Oregon, and California. My dad moved to southern California, and Sadie and I would sometimes visit him there. He was living in a bus that had been converted to a motorhome. We would stay in the back parking lot of a cafe in Dana Point, and my dad would give me a dollar to help with my sister and do her hair. We would play at parks and do things that didn't cost money. I could tell he missed living with us, even though it was a lot of work for him when we came to visit. I didn't realize it then, but I do appreciate now how hard it must have been for him to entertain us all day while living out of a motorhome. We did quality things, we were together, and that was all that mattered for my sister and me. I preferred to be with my dad over my mom at that younger age, so I didn't care or mind the rest. I cried so hard whenever it was time to go back to my mom. I couldn't understand the moving and the divide that their divorce had brought to our family.

When we visited my dad at his motorhome in southern California, he introduced Sadie and me to the beach-which was practically in our backyard. I had never seen the ocean before and fell in love with it right away. It was there in Dana Point that I declared out loud at 7 years of age that I would be a professional surfer someday! I started out "surfing" on a boogie board until my dad eventually bought me my own surfboard at a garage sale. From that time on, I was in the water as much as daylight, the tide, and my dad would allow. I was drawn into the water no matter how cold it might be, and was calmed and enamored by its movement and energy. For a little girl who so desperately craved stability and consistency, I think it's ironic that I was so drawn to the ocean with its turbulent power and unpredictable force. Perhaps through surfing I was somehow hoping to learn how to predict and control the seemingly unpredictable and uncontrollable. Or, maybe I just loved being alone in the water and leaving everyone and everything else behind on the land. I was more comfortable in the water than I was anywhere else. Whatever the motivation, I was beyond driven to the ocean and I worked relentlessly to master the art of surfing. I had found something to do that made me infinitely happier than anything else I had ever done in my short life. Yet, every time I found something that made me happy, it seemed only a matter of time before it somehow got tainted. My dad quickly found a way to take my love for surfing and turn it against me; to make me feel unworthy of his pride or even my own.

I begged my dad to let me enter a surf contest when I was still just learning to surf at about 9 years old. It was my very first contest, down at San Onofre State Beach, and I was nervous and definitely in over my head with the competition as well as with the size of the surf that day. I remember paddling out in my bikini and pink jersey, riding my candy-striped pink single-fin surfboard. I was a skinny little thing, a newcomer to WSSA competitions, feeling completely determined but also cautiously aware of the conditions. I remember catching two waves and riding them both to the beach. I quickly decided that it all felt too intense for me and I wanted to get out of the water. When I came to the shore, my dad came hustling down to the water's edge and asked me what the problem was. I said I was scared and that I wanted to get out. He said I was in second place and that I needed to get back out and finish! But I had just been held under by a strong wave and it got the best of me. I was no longer comfortable and just wanted to be done! He began to get angry and first tried his best to talk me back into the water, then threatened me, and finally dragged me back to the car in anger. And that is when I first acquired the "Quitter" nickname from him. He tore my leash off my leg and said he would never allow me to enter another contest again. He told me what an embarrassment I was to him, and nothing more than a quitter! There was no tempering the disappointment and sheer disgust he had for me. He told me I wasn't allowed to surf anymore and that I was a waste of his time and money. I didn't know what else to do, I felt helpless and was terrified of him at this point. We left the beach, and for months he referred to me only as "Quitter." I didn't enter another contest until I was 11 years old, and I knew that no matter how big or rough it ever got, no matter how huge a fall I took, I'd rather drown before I ever quit again! My dad humiliated and degraded me, but he also was the person who first taught me and supported me in my surfing. He also shared a love of baseball with me and we would play catch in the driveway for hours sometimes. These are gifts he gave me for which I am grateful.

Perhaps the only greater gift my dad ever gave me came in the form of Gini, a woman who I think of more like an angel. She was kind, beautiful, had herself together, and she sure loved my dad. I will never forget meeting Gini for the first time. Sadie and I walked excitedly up to the front door of her condo on Olinda Street in Dana Point. We fought over who would knock on the door, so of course I ran up fast to be the first to meet her. Gini answered the door with a huge, warm smile and I loved her in that moment. She welcomed us into her home and from then, she was family to me. She ran a preschool in nearby San Juan Capistrano and was naturally good with children. Gini and my dad married pretty fast and she immediately treated my sister and I as if we were her own-buying us beautiful clothing and showing us off to all her friends. She set up a nice bedroom for us, bought us matching sheets and comforters, and she even made me a collector of Cabbage Patch Kids! I really didn't even need all of that; I was just happy to have another home so that I did not need to go back to living with my mom. Gini and my dad belonged together and I had never seen him so happy. Even so, I remember times when he would push his luck with her. One time, I feared they might be on the verge of divorce and I went to Gini, afraid, and asked her to please take me with her if they were going to separate. She was secure, I could feel her love, and I preferred to be with her over my own biological parents. Thankfully, she and my dad worked things out; my dad would have missed me otherwise! I love Gini-Mom and I know that I wouldn't be where I am today if she had not come into our lives when she did.

There are many reasons why I love and am grateful for Gini- but none more than this: My baby sister, Karlee Malia. I was in love with this little girl from the moment I laid eyes on her. I actually have a picture that documents the first time I saw her. I think my dad took it. I was not quite nine years old, standing outside the nursery at San Clemente Hospital, looking in on her in the incubator. Gini had given birth via C-section and was still in recovery. I couldn't understand why my dad got to hold her and I didn't! I threw a good fit and then had to wait patiently for another couple days. When Gini and Karlee finally came through that door at home, I took hold of my baby sister and never let go. I would change her, sleep with her and was only willing to give her to Gini when she needed to nurse. She was mine and to this day, she still is. I loved Karlee and Sadie more than any other human beings on this earth until I eventually had the privilege of experiencing the love for my own children.

I lived with Gini and my dad permanently after Karlee was born. Sadie and I came into the world in a very different environment than Karlee. I had never felt safe or secure with my mom, and I knew my instincts were right when I realized the contrast of being loved and cared for by Gini. Gini came into my life and reaffirmed that something wasn't right with my mom. However, Sadie favored living with my mom during this time. It made me nervous to not be there with her. My mom had some interesting men in and out of her life and I always tried to scare them away when I went to visit. In one instance, she was furious when a male "friend" of hers tracked her down at work to let her know that her daughters had attacked him on the couch with a can of spray paint and then locked him out of our house. I would like to say that this was an isolated and outrageous incident, but I was ruthless and stopped at nothing when I felt my mom or her friends were putting my sister in danger.

    My mom and I obviously had serious differences because of the people she let into our home and other issues of this nature. My Mom has always been a good person, she just made poor decisions a lot of the time. Even with our differences, I always loved my Mom and wished better for her. Sadie was pretty quiet in general, and I could tell she was not the happiest little girl most of the time. But, we had fun when we were together and we always caused more trouble than four boys put together. We used to do incredibly naughty things to our neighbors. We destroyed property by mixing any and all liquids we could found in the garage into a bucket and then dumping our "potion" on the lawn of whomever we believed deserved it. We would even spell out curse words with it and it would burn whatever words we wrote into the grass. We would toilet paper people's homes and use Hefty bags to tie people's front doors closed so they were trapped in their homes. Sadie and I admittedly did many naughty things, but in our own way we would bond as sisters over plotting, executing, and rehashing our escapades. Without any real parental oversight at my mom's house, we were expected to regulate our own behavior and our neighbors certainly suffered when we failed to do so. Even though I look back now and feel bad for any lasting or harmful effects of our actions, I have to be honest and admit that some of my greatest childhood memories simply came from making trouble in the neighborhood with Sadie.

    I continued to live primarily with Gini and my dad in southern California, with occasional visits to my mom, as well as frequent visits to family and friends on the Island of Kauai with my dad. My mom eventually spiraled downward with her addictions and Sadie eventually came to live with us in California when I was about ten years old. I felt a distant sense of worry for my mom now living all alone, but was mostly just relieved to finally have the peace of knowing both of my sisters were with me every day.

My passion for surfing seemed to grow over the years, but it seemed I could also quickly pick up the fundamentals for just about any sport. I was blessed with an athletic ability and was always actively involved in team sports whether through formal leagues or just playing out in the streets. I preferred playing on boys' teams as much as possible. I played baseball or Little League with the boys for many years before finally playing softball with other girls when I got to high school. The years I played in Little League afforded me a great boost in my confidence. I had one coach, Bruce Whittaker, who always believed in me and made me feel like I could do anything regardless of my gender. He would tell me that I was faster, stronger, and better than any of the boys out there and without fail he chose me to play on his team year after year. I thank him to this day for the confidence he had in me and the confidence it instilled in me as well. As I look back on all the coaches I have had, he is one who truly helped to shape me as a person and player from an early age and for that I am grateful. It's a true gift when you are in a position and have the power to influence and guide the life of another person in a positive direction. Even now, I keep his model in mind when I coach Little League myself, in hopes that I can encourage and inspire even one young athlete to believe in himself the way Coach Whittaker once encouraged and inspired me.

    I continued to pursue surfing with passion and devotion. I was determined to become a professional surfer, and I tried to get out in the water every single day. Because he knew how much I loved surfing, my dad would threaten to or actually take away my surfboard for any real or perceived violation of his rules or his respect. He was strict with me to the point of ridiculousness. I would get in serious trouble, serious meaning month-long restrictions at a time. He would make me sit in the office until school started, go to class, sit back in the office at lunch time, and then after school I would go sit in Gini's preschool office until 6 or 7pm when he was off work. I would also have to write sentences about whatever I had done. He would tell me to write 500 sentences-thinking it would take me a week. Instead, I would get them done in one day and proudly present them to him only for him to get madder and tell me to write 5,000 more. He found painful and humiliating ways to treat me that were completely uncalled for and I eventually hated him for it. I felt like I was never good enough and like I couldn't make him proud of me. I felt so "bad" in his eyes. He was so unbelievable and stubborn. I felt like he never appreciated what a good kid I was or how hard I tried for him. It took me time to realize that this behavior reflected him, not me.

In spite of the many issues with my dad, I was finally feeling relatively steady and secure when I started high school in Dana Point. I felt in command of my life and that I was finally responsible for my own self and doing just fine. I was excelling in my classes, making friends, and I had been the only freshman to make the varsity softball team. I was also gaining great experience and exposure on the school's surf team. I started to work various jobs to cover my own expenses and even bought my own car. I needed to feel and truly be independent because I didn't believe I could count on anyone else to take care of me. No matter the age or circumstance, I always felt that I was on my own at a young age, like an adult in a kid's body. It was all I ever knew and honestly all I still know today. As a teenager, that reality forced me to work harder because I didn't have the safety net that most other kids my age had. I suspect I actually dodged a lot of bad habits because of that.

The harder I worked, the more I saw my dreams becoming a reality. I was finally feeling that I might be able to grasp that elusive sense of stability I had always craved. And, then, Gini and my dad made the decision to move the family to Kauai. Although I loved Kauai, I was charging down a planned path of success in my mind and that path did not entail another disruption to my life! It didn't matter what I thought, though; I was crushed and knew I had no choice. I was certainly still considering other options in the back of my mind (like running away!), but a few days before we were scheduled to move, I woke to find my car had been stolen in the night. I have always suspected this was not just a simple coincidence. No matter the situation, I knew that I would have to go to Kauai with my family and make the best of it and hope to just somehow get back to California as quickly as possible.

Kauai is the most beautiful place on earth in my mind and also in my heart. I love Kauai, and to this day, I feel at home there. Spending time growing up there as a teenager made me stronger and helped me see the beauty in nature, the power in the ocean, and the grace in people who don't have much. It has a feel and energy all its own. The waves are always good enough to paddle out, and being there took my surfing to a new level. There are places to surf on Kauai that you can be in the water and turn toward the beach to see waterfalls on a mountain in the distance. It's a magical place and a spiritual one. I have lifelong friends, family and some of my best memories on Kauai.

In spite of the almost mystical properties of Kauai for my spirits and my soul (and my surfing!), my differences with my dad only escalated after we moved there. I got good grades, was a standout athlete, and wasn't experimenting with alcohol, boys, or drugs like so many of the other kids. I appreciated that my dad cared enough to punish me for certain things--but he always took it too far and by doing so, lost my respect. I was fearful of him, not respectful. Big difference. He would yell and punish, but would never listen, understand, or explain. There was no room for me to ever make even the slightest mistake, and this eventually came between us. This is something I have never forgotten and it took me a long time to forgive. Looking back now, he was always operating from ego with me, as if he was scared to love me too much or with his whole heart. There were many things that I had tried to block out, to forgive, and to forget with him. Let me be clear that the differences between my dad and me are immense. The older I got, and the more perspective I gained, the harder it became for me to even look at him-much less respect him. Although I have tried to share my story honestly, I have left out many details to protect the already fragile dynamics of my family. Suffice to say that eventually my dad hurt and humiliated me in every possible way. I was old enough to know what was okay and what was not and I was no longer able to stifle my feelings of resentment toward him. I faced those issues, I faced him, and I moved forward. There are some things I think a daughter can quite possibly never understand, but it takes strength to at least acknowledge those ugly things we bring along as baggage on our life journey. He tried to control me and dominate me, and the more I would fight back, the more I would eventually suffer for it. I knew that the damage he had done to our relationship was irreparable and I wasn't willing to play the role of his victim any longer. The stronger I became and the more defiant I was, the more he seemed to loathe me. His anger and my own seemed to intensify until I was truly worried about what could happen if we continued to live under the same roof.

No matter how great my love for my sisters, I now felt that they would be okay and possibly even better off without me there to antagonize my dad. I never felt that they were in the same dangers with my dad as I was. I finally made the difficult decision to leave the safety of my family and home on Kauai. My boyfriend, Kasey, was a professional surfer and he helped get me a plane ticket so I could go back to the life I missed in southern California. After a major fight with my dad and Gini I eventually got out of the house and on the plane by myself. At seventeen years old, I was ready to be independent and on my own; in charge of my own destiny. I was definitely scared, but I was relieved to know I would not be my dad's victim or verbal punching bag any longer. My departure from Kauai was monumental in that it marked the end of any type of dependence on my biological parents. When I left the island that day, I truly left behind any expectation of a traditional parent-child relationship altogether and I knew I was legitimately on my own. I felt that I had been an adult in a child's body for so many years already, and I knew I was ready to be free to pursue my own happiness without my dad acting as a human roadblock. He always told me never to allow anyone to stand in the way of accomplishing my goals. Funny enough, he was the only one who ever tried. He was the very first man to violate me, betray me, break my heart, disappoint me, and let me down.

In spite of all this, I still look back on my childhood with no regrets. Of course, I sometimes wonder where I would be if my parents had been positively engaged in my life and had been the support a child should be able to expect of her parents. Now that I'm a parent myself, I can't imagine the pain of missing out on my kids' lives for any amount of time or finding out that they never felt secure or safe in my care. I couldn't imagine finding out that they felt like burdens and unloved at times. I can't imagine any greater pain in my heart—besides losing them altogether—than that. I just have to believe that my parents gave whatever they were capable of at that point in time. I have forgiven the past and am committed to living so much in the moment that I rarely think of what they didn't do right until something in my life now reflects a past wound.

I try to stay positive and reflect on the gifts that my parents did give me. My dad brought many of my greatest loves into my life: My sisters, the ocean, surfing, and sports. He taught me to never give up and to never quit. He taught me to stand up for myself and eventually to walk away when a bond is beyond repair. I might have preferred to learn these lessons in very different manners, but I think it's fair to give him credit for helping to shape me into the person I am today. I love him for the gifts and for the times I know he did his honest best. Forgiveness isn't always easy, yet it can be a powerful gift you might actually give to yourself when you give it to another. I am grateful for having learned this, and it has been a humbling lesson to live by for sure. Although I have tried to forgive, I have never again relied upon or trusted my father for anything.

As for my mom, I learned many lessons from her as well. While my dad was aggressive and hostile, my best assessment of my mother is that she was simply immature and unintentionally neglectful. In spite of her very physical approach to discipline, I don't believe she ever had the intention of being cruel to Sadie or me. I wish that she and my dad had at least learned to disagree and work things out so that she could have helped model conflict resolution for us girls. Disagreeing with those we love is a normal part of any relationship. But, to hurt people with your words and hands is an awful life lesson for impressionable young daughters to observe in their mother. I didn't realize how unexpectedly I could grow up and find myself not far from some of those very situations. If only by modeling what not to do, my mom did give me that gift of helping me look back to similar moments in my childhood and remember the negative influence it had; the fear and insecurity I felt. It has not always been the easy or natural choice for me, but I have always found the power to choose differently whenever my own children are involved. We have choices in life to repeat that which we already know is not right and then try to make excuses for it--or we can take a stand and do something different altogether. Perhaps I didn't give my mom the chance she deserved to try to love me and raise me when I chose to live with my dad and Gini so many years ago. However, I made the best choices I knew as a child and I simply can't recall happy or positive memories with her in my early life.

The childhood memories included here simply reflect how I perceived, processed, and now remember things from my own life. I know that memories can be flimsy and even fallible, and I am sure my parents have their own versions of their roles in my childhood. But, this is my story. And in my story, my father never again played any meaningful role after I left his home on Kauai at age seventeen. I am thankful, though, that I will have the opportunity to write about my mom again in future chapters. Her story and evolution as a person does not end here, and neither does mine.

Chapter Two

"GROWING UP"

When I left Kauai for my life of independence back in California, I had very little money, only a handful of possessions, and absolutely no real plans. I thought a lot about my Grandpa Sam and his wife, Judi, who lived in Dana Point right near my old high school. I loved my Grandpa Sam beyond words and his would have been the first and most logical choice in any search for a stable and loving home. Unfortunately, my dad had warned me repeatedly to leave my grandparents alone; saying that only a Taker and Leech would take advantage of them in such a way. I heeded his warning—in part because I believed he was right, and also because I knew that living with his dad would prevent me from completely severing ties with my own dad. This is one of the few significant regrets of my life thus far; that I let the ugly words of one miserable person keep me away from one of the most beautiful souls I have ever known. I can only imagine how different things might have been if I had allowed myself to admit that I needed the love and support of someone else and to reach out and ask for that. Looking back now, I know that Grandpa Sam would surely have given me the stability I needed during such a tumultuous phase in my life. I believed I was being strong and independent by not asking for help, but it would have taken much more strength and courage for me to admit my weaknesses, my loneliness, and to reach out to someone who would have loved me best of all. Sadly, I lost that opportunity because I was still letting my dad have the power and control over my thoughts and my choices.

Firm in my decision not to engage my grandparents in my issues, I took Kasey up on his offer to help me get on my feet. In addition to buying me the plane ticket to California, Kasey also convinced his parents to let me stay with them until I could get myself situated somewhere else. They lived in the most beautiful house I quite possibly had ever seen and for certain had ever been in. His parents welcomed me to their home and made me feel included. His father, Bob, taught me about God and the love of Jesus. He was always happy to spend time with me and I would sometimes just ride along with him to meetings or to run errands. Kasey's stepmother, Susan, became my favorite surf buddy. I loved spending time with them both, and I also ended up helping them a bit with their younger kids. It was the least I could do in exchange for their hospitality. After getting settled into their home, I was immediately focused on making sure I got back into school as soon as possible and also finding a job to cover my living expenses.

I quietly forged my way back into my old high school by lying about my address (since Kasey's address in San Clemente was zoned for a different high school). I found a job hosting at a restaurant and would also work at Salt Creek beach in the early mornings, answering the phones and giving the daily surf report. (It's possible that I might have been known to stretch the truth and downplay the water conditions to the callers sometimes, just so that we didn't have a rush of surfers in the water when our school surf team was practicing!)

As time went by, I came to feel that I was overstaying my welcome at Kasey's parents' house. I know they would not ever have kicked me out on the street, but I could feel that my presence wasn't as welcome anymore. Kasey and I were also having those typical issues that were innocent enough but that seem to plague many teen relationships. It felt like the logical time for me to move along; I couldn't pay rent and I surely had no business living in a mansion. My dad's words resonated in my head and I became consumed with the idea that I was a Taker and a Leach. I eventually thanked Bob and Susan for their immeasurable hospitality and acted as if I had somewhere else to go.

I was too proud to ask for help from anyone else. My dad had made it clear that if I asked for help, I was burdening people. He always was good at having a name to call me that was low and condescending. I believed every word he said and I stayed clear of people that I now know would have been perfectly happy to have had the chance to help me. He manipulated me into thinking I truly was a selfish Loser. I was afraid to let others get too close, for fear that they would also realize that truth about me. Even in my dire straits, I acted like things were simply perfect in my life. I became an expert at distorting my reality to other people.

Before I knew it, I found myself spending nights at the Doheny beach campground. I snuck in most nights after dark to set up a tent and sleeping bag that I had quietly "borrowed" out of Grandpa Sam's garage. I always wore a hoodie sweatshirt and was careful not to alert to the fact that I was a young girl walking in alone to a campground after dark. I became hypersensitive and very aware of my surroundings. There were other homeless people there, mostly men, and I'm pretty certain there were not any other teenage girls sleeping there alone. I was scared at times of being attacked or raped in the night, but I was also quite comfortable in some ways because I was just happy that I wasn't burdening anybody in the world. All things considered, I was actually okay.

I would wake up at the campground before daylight every morning and head to Salt Creek beach where surf team practices were held. From there I would head to the women's locker room to clean up and get ready for school. The female janitor saw me there one day, waiting outside the locker room before it was even light out. She took the time to ask me if I was okay. She probably thought that I had gotten in a fight with my parents in the night prior and had maybe just left the house early. When I decided to be honest and tell her of my circumstances, she promised to keep my secret and asked how she could help. From that day on, she would meet me every weekday morning and let me use the hot shower and facilities. She would sometimes also clean my jeans or shirt, and help me with things of that nature. Those small favors were monumental to me. I have never forgotten her kindness or her generosity. I look back and reflect on this sweet stranger and am reminded of the power we all have to touch a life of another through simple acts of kindness.

I continued with this routine at the campground for a couple months, until one day I was called into the office at school to discuss the address on my registration form. The administrator said that my school was getting some pressure from a neighboring high school whose surf team wanted to prove I was living outside the legal zone for my school. Kasey's house in San Clemente, where they apparently thought I was still staying, fell outside of the boundaries to attend the school in Dana Point. My school demanded a valid address and I was forced with no choice but to tell the truth about my homelessness. I was sent out of the office and told that I would be dis-enrolled from school because district guidelines were clear that enrollment required both a valid address and parent or guardian supervision.

I couldn't believe that I was being kicked out of school for being homeless. The administration didn't offer to help me in any way. They just expected me to move along and figure something out. Most kids would have been relieved and happy, but I had a plan for college. Without high school, there would be no college. I seriously couldn't believe these people! They didn't care about my circumstances, they only cared that their rules were complied with and that I had proper address on paper and someone who would accept responsibility for me. I had no proper address and nobody to accept responsibility for me except for myself. I left the office that day crying, discouraged, and overwhelmed. Feeling deflated and alone, I ran into Damian, my dearest childhood friend from Little League, and one of my few trusted friends. Even Damian thought I was still living at Kasey's house. I told him what was really going on, and that I was humiliated and afraid that I would be judged and teased for being a bum. I explained that due to politics with surfing, the school had found out I was not living within their boundaries. Damian promised not to tell anyone-not even his parents-and he insisted that he would be sneaking me into his room at night. Damian was worried and protective of me and was nothing less than an angel when I needed one most. I went back to the office with Damian at my side and said I would be living with his family. We put his address on the registration sheet and said we would have the paper back the next day with the documents signed by his parents. You can be sure we had already done much worse than forge signatures!

Starting that night, Damian would sneak me into his house to sleep. I would leave before sunrise each day in order to bypass his parents and would head to surf team and to the locker room at the beach. We were always like brother and sister-no funny business at all. I would sleep at the opposite end of his bed, not even under the covers, so that if his parents came in they would see that we weren't up to anything inappropriate under their roof. I slept in my clothes because I didn't even have pajamas. I was safe. I wasn't the girl they needed to worry about! Damian was busy with plenty of others and was clever about it when it came to them. One morning, Damian's mom came in before we woke up, and she was understandably very upset to find me there. I remember the look on her face and her obvious disappointment and discomfort at my presence. I felt my Dad's words resonating through my body and could hear them echoing in my head…"Leach, Loser, Taker, User…" It was awful. I was embarrassed and immediately left as quickly as I could. I can only remember apologizing profusely while I grabbed my backpack and left. I cried so hard that morning in fear I had gotten Damian in trouble and that his parents would hate me. I just couldn't handle the fear and anxiety of thinking that one more person was judging me or thinking less of me. When Damian found me at school later that day, he said his parents wanted me to come back to the house for dinner that evening.

When I showed up to dinner as requested, I was ashamed and embarrassed beyond words. His parents, John and Diane, were kind but firm. They made sure that I understood that sleeping in Damian's room was totally inappropriate. They asked me a lot of questions about my situation, about my parents, and whether Bob and Susan knew that when I left their house I had nowhere else to go. They asked me about school, work, and everything really. I honestly don't remember much about my answers, except that I told them the truth. I wasn't sure what they thought--besides the very clear fact that I would not be sleeping in Damian's room anymore! They finally told me not to lie to them again; that I could be honest and trust them. They invited me to stay in their guest room downstairs. I remember feeling so excited, yet equally terrible, for accepting their offer. They invited me to have dinner with them nightly when I wasn't working and emphasized that all of the house rules would apply to me while under their roof.

These were rules I knew Damian barely followed, but that I would never break. I wanted to be perfect for them and as if I wasn't even there.

The first night I was there "legally," I cried myself to sleep--half in relief and half in guilt for letting myself burden Damian's family. I stayed in a room that housed Diane's beautiful homemade quilts and some of their miscellaneous objects were stored there in boxes. I kept my few belongings and my backpack on a chair in the corner. Their two Rottweilers, Fridge and Addy, slept with me at night. It was so comforting to be around dogs again, and most importantly, not to be alone. The dogs were beautiful and welcoming, loudly snoring at times and then growling when I would try to move them over so that my own feet or legs might fit. I felt that they loved me, but this was probably just because no one else allowed them to sleep in bed with them! Rottweilers are convincing and manipulative. They are funny, strong, sensitive and civil. Because of Fridge and Addy, I have had a Rottweiler as a pet for most of my adult life so far.

The next morning, John came into my room very early with a homemade smoothie. I knew he did this every morning for Damian and his sister and I thought it was a sweet gesture that he had made one for me on this day also. I was so grateful, and I can remember sitting on the edge of the bed that I had already made, not sure what to think. It was the best smoothie and yet I felt so bad that John probably felt obligated to make me one. I was so nervous to go out of the room, to go upstairs, or anywhere at all. I didn't know if I should use the shower, or if I should exit through the front door or just keep using the back door that I had been sneaking out of all along. I didn't want to dirty their towels, make noise, or even take up space. No matter their hospitality, I felt like a Taker; even though I was really taking nothing.

    I can still remember sitting on the bed, drinking that smoothie and apprehensive to even move in any direction. I eventually just took the empty glass upstairs and forced myself to use the front door when I exited. I headed to surf team and then to shower as usual at the locker room. This became my new norm and it felt good. I asked John and Diane if they wanted me to pay them something for staying there, but they said they just wanted me to be comfortable. And I was.

    John and Diane eventually had to officially sign for me at the school. They became my legal guardians and I felt as though I was officially part of their family. Damian and I called ourselves "brother" and "sister" and we introduced ourselves as such to anyone new that we met. It was always that way and still is today. Despite our physical differences, we were like twins and we absolutely drove the poor parents nuts. John visited the principal's office on more than one occasion that year, sometimes for me, sometimes for Damian, and sometimes for both of us at once. Damian and I had no shortage of fun, but lived different lives a lot of the time because I worked two jobs and maintained myself financially. I bought a car from John and Diane, paid my own insurance, gas, pager, school supplies and clothing. John and Diane gave me what money couldn't buy: A home and healthy attention.

    I continued to be pretty successful at balancing many varied demands on my time. I would get my homework done, manage to work multiple jobs, and be a standout athlete. I somehow managed to be on the varsity basketball, surfing, softball, and track teams. I was endlessly energetic and always the class clown no doubt. I tried to be kind to everyone, but like most teenagers I did have my share of issues of feeling like I didn't fit in, didn't have nice things like the other girls, and I was teased and bullied at times for that. I had friends in all different groups, mostly because I played an array of different sports. I was definitely a jock, but also a surfer, so the crossover of these different groups of friends never allowed me to totally belong to any of them. This was good for me, because it allowed for me to kind of float around anonymously. I was comfortable knowing that nobody could close the distance in on me to know what my life was really like. No matter the circumstances, I was doggedly focused on my surfing career, a future in collegiate sports, and just my future in general. I was determined to maximize my potential and was driven even then to get things done and done right.

I walked around like all was perfect in the world and in my life. It most certainly was not, and looking back now there are elements that were downright scary. When I think back to high school, the timeline and order of events are honestly a blur. Between my two high schools in Kauai and California, the memories overlap and intertwine and I can't always tease apart my age or grade when certain things happened. When I actually sat down and tried to work it out on paper how and what I did, or when I did it, nothing seems to work out. All I know is I just did! I just kept moving forward…one homework assignment…one surfing session...one softball practice...one work shift... one day at a time. I always lived very much in the moment. I tried to take on everything life dealt me with an open heart and brave soul. Always fighting back against the challenges and my own personal demons that would arise from time to time, I would do the only thing I knew and dig in deep like the warrior I felt I was. Looking back, I actually think I was tougher then than I am now!

As tough as I felt or tried to be, sometimes all a person wants is to feel loved and valued and understood. Even though I wouldn't allow myself to burden my Grandpa Sam, I sought him out often and he never failed to make me feel exactly that-loved and valued and understood. There wasn't a time he looked at me and didn't have that certain grin that belonged only to me. Even when I knew he wasn't impressed with something I had done, he still was consistent with that grin and for that, I was always willing to share my everything with him openly and honestly. I shared my friends with him, my secrets, and some of my demons. It never mattered who I brought over--prim and proper friends or ones that were tattooed from head to toe--he greeted each and every one with a smile, a hug, and a warm welcome to his home. It seems that everyone who ever knew my Grandpa felt like I did around him. There were even times that I would pull up to his house to find my own friends there visiting with him and Judi without me! He was unconditional in his love for everyone and he always supported me without judgment.

Grandpa Sam and Judi were open and generous to everyone, and they often had someone living in their home that needed shelter or help along the way of their own journey. My grandfather was a diabetic, but he never complained about his health or anything else. One funny thing about him in my mind is that he apparently liked to walk around naked. I never saw him naked, but I would often hear about it from the neighbors-which I thought was hilarious. Judi would laugh all the time when I would tell her that this neighbor or that neighbor had seen him through the window in the mornings, just standing right there for anyone to see.

My Grandpa and Judi had a peaceful relationship. They were best friends and lovers in one. My Grandpa spoke of her with such admiration and respect. Judi had to have surgery for a brain aneurysm and when she went in to the hospital, my Grandpa Sam fell apart. He said he simply wouldn't be okay if anything were to happen to her. I had never seen him cry or heard him scared at all, so this was a first. He only cried one other time that I knew of, and that was when Nugget, their rescued golden retriever mix got sick and passed away. My Grandpa, Judi, and even I loved that dog. Nugget and I would play so hard and although my Grandpa laughed hysterically, Judi would get so mad at me sometimes. She especially hated when I would draw on Nugget's face with Sharpie pen. My Grandpa laughed the hardest when I drew horns and a devil's mustache on him. He was trying to get the ink off, rubbing his face all over the carpet and Judi went ballistic on me. I would feel bad on some level for upsetting Judi, but couldn't hold back the laughter and even tears at times thinking it was so funny and especially with my Grandpa egging me on.

  My Grandpa always made me feel happy and at peace. I used to come to his house in my bikini when it was raining out and take naps on the couch in between my surfing sessions. He would always warn me of the chances of catching a cold, but then would follow his words with "You know what you're doing and I won't be the one to tell you not to have fun!" He nurtured me and looked out for me, but he also got me, accepted me and let me be me. Even though I didn't spend as much time with my Grandpa Sam as I would have liked, in large part due to the words of my father, just knowing I had his love went a long way and carried me through times when I would otherwise have felt very alone. His attention and love for me were unconditional and no matter what I did right or wrong, these never seemed to fluctuate or diminish.

One of my proudest memories was when my Grandpa Sam showed up to the Oceanside river jetties to watch me compete at the California State Finals for surfing. I remember feeling totally intimidated that morning and feeling a sort of pressure of being the favorite who was just expected to win--which had me feeling a little unnerved. I loved to compete and get out and fight for my place at each and every competition and never liked to let the pressure of others' expectations factor in to my mindset. For something as big as this, though, the talk and attention were seeming to dominate the surfing itself. The conditions were fair that day, but I never really liked surfing the jetties. I had invited my Grandpa Sam to see me surf for the first time, but I wasn't sure if he would make it there. When I saw him walk onto that beach, my heart jumped and I knew I would simply have to win and I would win for him. He had heard so much of me surfing, seen me all wet and sandy running through his house in my bikini, but he had never seen me actually get out on the waves and surf.

This was my biggest contest to date and I was so proud to have my Grandpa Sam there supporting me. Once the competition got underway, I remember looking up to find him after each and every wave, and without exception I would see that same proud grin across his face. I did have a great day and did well out on the waves and won the California State Title. But, the best part for me was that I knew that he wouldn't have cared what I did that day--he was proud of me always and for just being me. I know I would have seen the exact same proud grin on his face no matter how I performed. When it was all over and I had the chance to hug Grandpa Sam and thank him for being there, he was beaming and I know that he was beyond proud of me. And, I was beyond happy to have him there to witness such an important event in my life. No matter how successful I had been in my other athletic competitions, I was always painfully aware that I never had family in the stands or on the shores to support me. Having my Grandpa Sam there for me made an already exciting day a day to remember for a lifetime--less so for the title that I won and more for the pride I felt in showing him that I was a winner like he had always believed me to be. I asked him if he would surf with me sometime and he said he would.

Surfing was my number one priority in high school and still is an important part of my life today. From the time I first put my toes in the water as a young girl, I knew the ocean had changed me and would be part of my life forever. I was relentless for sure, and worked hard consistently. I got my first surf sponsorships when I was about 15 years old from Killer Dana and Arnette Sunglasses. Killer Dana was a little surf shop on Pacific Coast Highway in Dana Point that was owned by two guys named Chris and Gary. They started me off with t-shirts and wax for my surfboard, and they later helped me with surfboards as well. I watched them grow over time and they watched me grow. Today they are a respected local shop in the same location, with a recognizable brand name known worldwide. The team at Killer Dana believed in me at a young age, and just knowing this motivated me to be better. They gave me a job when I needed it and they were always there to support me as a surfer and as a person.

Martial arts first became a part of my life during my senior year of high school. I have no idea how I fit in, but a friend of mine from school invited me to a class and I loved it. My first class was an Okinawan Shuri-Ryu Karate class in Laguna Beach, and I was hooked from that day on. I trained about 12 hours a week next to my already insanely busy high school schedule. I loved doing Katas. Karate "Kata" is a Japanese word describing detailed patterns of movements that can be practiced either solo or in pairs. Each Kata is a complete fight system, with the movements and postures being a living reference guide to the correct form and structure of the technique used within that system. The moves are executed while visualizing the enemy attacks and their responses. I would lose myself in these forms, peacefully working hard to perfect each position and the flow and timing.

I can vividly remember that I would sometimes go visit my Grandpa Sam and ask him and Judi to watch me run through my Katas the night before a Karate tournament. They would sit there together on the couch, straight-faced and sincere, as I bowed into my imaginary ring in the living room and proceed to kick ass on five different imaginary people. I would have died laughing if I were them. However, they would sit there and silently watch and support me, taking it just as seriously as I did. My grandfather would tell me how good it looked and then ask me a ton of questions about each position. Whether he was sincerely interested or not, he would sure make me feel important and confident for my tournament the next day.

    I loved having Karate in my life, and I felt that I was honing my skills on the outside to match the warrior I felt I was on the inside. I was not going to live in fear if ever I found myself sleeping in a campground again or facing threats from my dad. I was being proactive, productive, and also bettering myself physically. I was always tough, but I had never been trained. I thought like an athlete and knew the power and functionality I would gain if I trained and polished my skills. I don't know how to pursue a passion half-heartedly, so of course I eventually joined the competitive team. I only got to the level of purple belt, but I won a California State Championship at the USKA that first year and a few more after that. Karate helped me find qualities in myself that I respected. I worked hard and knew that I earned and deserved any of the accolades that came along with my passionate pursuit for mastery. However, I eventually became so busy with my many other commitments and interests in life that I simply stopped practicing karate altogether.

As passionately as I believed in myself in some areas like surfing and other athletics, I also doubted in myself in other areas and walked away from what could have been some extraordinary opportunities because of that self-doubt. Most young girls would likely agree that being nominated for Homecoming Queen of her class would be a sincere honor. To have your physical and/or inner beauty recognized by your peers is special and a true compliment indeed. It should be pretty clear by now, though, that I was not the stereotypical teenage girl, so having a stereotypical teen girl honor bestowed on me felt odd indeed. My name was somehow in the mix of girls that had been nominated and I was suddenly aware of myself and how I physically looked to others. People often told me I was pretty, or had beautiful eyes, but I never really had any interest in my appearance. I was very comfortable in my own skin, probably because I had grown up in a bikini and didn't really think of my body as much more than a vehicle for all the sports and surfing I did. I went to school in my surf team shirts, jeans, "boy clothes," and the Killer Dana surf t-shirts that I was always proud to wear. Given the near total lack of thought I gave to my physical appearance I was blindsided to find that I was now being considered for the Homecoming Court.

The school held a mandatory meeting for the female nominees. I was very hesitant about the whole process, but decided to keep an open mind and I attended the meeting. The first thing I heard was that we would need to ask our fathers to accompany us in the Homecoming parade. We were expected to have a formal dress and shoes, of course, as well as proper hair and makeup, and a corsage for both father and daughter. I was beyond intimidated. I felt nervous and didn't want to tell any of these people about my situation, or the very real fact that I didn't meet any of the school's requirements. When the meeting was over, I stayed after to talk to the teacher about why I would not participate. At the last second, I reconsidered and asked a silly question instead, and left without really talking to her. I remember going home that evening and deciding not to even tell John or Diane. I couldn't burden them with anything. Asking John to walk me would have been an honor for him. I can see this now, but back then, all I could hear in my head was my dad's voice.

Being in the running for the Homecoming Court meant the nominees had to attend various activities in order to generate votes and school spirit. This consoled me a bit because I didn't have a particular group of people that I hung out with and who would rally up votes for me within our social circle. I was an athlete, and the athletes never won, so I felt pretty confident I was safe from being voted the winner. I thought to myself that I would just wait for the right time to fake being sick or find some other creative way to get out of it. This was really stressful for me for some reason, and I felt detached from it all as I watched the girls gather votes and talk excitedly about their dresses, shoes, and the big night. It was exciting for many, but not for me. I didn't want to be exposed or have any attention. I was content how things were and I didn't want to rock the boat in any direction for fear of being completely overturned.

There was a final committee meeting the week of the Homecoming event. The votes had been tallied, and the court would be announced at the football game that weekend. We were required to bring our dresses in for approval from the teacher overseeing the event, and to get our final directions for the big night. When I showed up late and with no dress in hand, the teacher looked at me a bit irritated. I remember not knowing what to say or how to start saying it. My face was hot and I couldn't look at her. I started off by saying that I was too shy and that I had changed my mind. Then, I started crying halfway through my excuses and lies and she finally stopped me. In a very calm voice, she said: "Look at me! You ARE the Homecoming Queen, Danielle Martin. None of this talk is an option at this point. You are the first athlete that's ever been elected! So stop being shy and go get your dress!"

I wasn't really even the slightest bit shy, and of course I also had no dress to go and get. I finally had to look her straight in the eye and tell her that I didn't have a father to walk me, a dress or shoes, nor money for flowers and all the other requirements. I was crying hard now, with my hands over my face, nothing short of humiliated and embarrassed. I wanted to be invisible. I wanted her to understand and let me off the hook, but I also think I desperately wanted her to hear my inaudible plea that she find a way to help me. Instead, she consoled me and told me she wished she had known earlier so that she could have found a way to help. She agreed to release me from the court and said that the honor would go to the next girl who had probably worked hard to get votes, had her father to walk her with pride and money to buy a beautiful dress and shoes.

The cool thing is that the girl who did win was also an athlete.

As hurt and upset as I was, I left there with less stress and a sense of relief that I can't explain to this day. It was an awful feeling to know I was willingly walking away from what should have been the classic teenage dream, but it was also a sweet relief. Like other times in my life, before and since, something that should have been an incredible honor or accomplishment was marred by the negative thoughts in my head and my inability to believe that I was worthy of true love and recognition.

I went the next night and watched the ceremony for a little bit on my way to work. Instead of wearing a beautiful gown, I was in my work uniform. I watched alone from a distance as the girls on the Homecoming Court rode around the track with their dads in convertible old-fashioned cars. The Homecoming Queen, Ursula, was beautiful and I am sure she felt loved and accepted. I felt sad and empty beyond words as I watched from afar, but still relieved to have the safety of my relative anonymity. I was scared for people to really see me, to really notice me, for fear they would see what my dad saw in me-and what he made me see in myself. Had I found the strength then to love and believe in myself, to give myself the chance to be loved and adored by others, it would have been a very different night and this a very different story.

Looking back, I can see that I was just too proud to reach out to John and Diane. I should have at least given them-and more importantly, myself-the opportunity to be part of something so memorable. I have no doubt now that John and Diane would have been honored to support me with the Homecoming Court. I honestly just did not feel good about myself, deep inside, and didn't feel like I deserved to be on the same stage as those other pretty and popular girls. From my vantage point, they had it all and I would only feel like a bum alongside them. I reflect back on that time and know now how sad it is to have felt such stress over that kind of privilege and honor. My peers believed I was worthy of recognition, but I just did not believe it about myself.

This wasn't the only time that I let my self-doubt get the best of me. Prom came along, and I was asked to go with a dear friend, Matt Clements. Kasey was still my boyfriend at the time, but he was no longer in high school and preferred that I go with a friend from my surf team. Matt was the sweetest guy in school and always my biggest fan. I was working at the time for a swimsuit company called "Raisins, Roxy and Radio Fiji" as a fit model. What this meant is that they used my body as their standard when designing their swimsuits. I would stand there, a living mannequin of sorts, so that the seamstress could adjust all the straps and seams to my body-which is what they used for their size Medium standard. I was chatting about prom and my indecision about going, and they offered to help me out. Their company made swim suit cover ups, and some of them were pretty cool. They offered me on that was floor length, black mesh "dress" with a stripe down the sides. It was no prom dress, but it was free and it would do! I complemented it with an old pair of Converse tennis shoes and called it a day.

On the big night of the prom, I once again had mixed emotions. It was a special night, and I was proud of myself for pulling together a dress of any kind without having to ask for help. I owned it, and was happy to be there in that classic high school moment. But, as I lined up with the others in front of Damian's garage, while the parents took obligatory pictures, I felt like a scrub alongside the other girls in their traditional gowns and heels. Looking at the picture makes me a little sad even today. I was trying so hard to be strong, to not be a Taker. I wish I had reached out to Diane and asked her to help me be like all the other girls for just that one night. I think I was also sad or disappointed on some level that Diane couldn't see that I needed someone to mother me and nurture me-just as much as I needed the food, bed, and roof they so graciously shared.

It's probably a good thing I wasn't crowned Homecoming Queen or even Prom Princess, because my behavior was not always what you would expect of royalty. Even with all my commitments to sports, surf, work, and school, I found plenty of time to cause trouble with Damian and our other buddies, Scooter, Chris and Phil. We tormented the school and teachers and just did whatever made us laugh. We conjured up some awful things to do, and on weekends we would go around in one of our cars causing relatively innocent trouble. I can't deny that it was fun. Soaping water fountains, toilet papering houses of those that did us wrong, pulling pranks on the school campus when it was closed, breaking into abandoned houses…We were fun and we were funny--just ask us! I am sure that nobody thought we were as funny as we did.

With our high school graduation on the horizon, we started collecting tennis balls from wherever we could find them in anticipation of a senior prank. We saved the balls by the hundreds in huge trash bags that we hid in the mechanics workshop area where Damian took class. We took our time and we were strategic. Looking back, we were even brilliant as a matter of fact, considering the calculation required for the collection, stealth in the storage, and careful execution of this prank.

Our school had a mall area that was two stories high. Students would come through this mall between classes or when walking to their lockers. So, on no particular day at the end of our senior year, Damian, Chris, Scooter, Phil and I left our respective third period classes early. We met at the mechanic shop and took the bags of tennis balls up to the second floor. We divided up between the four corners of the mall, and when students began flooding the area, we ripped the bags open and began dumping the balls off the balcony. I remember Damian and I running downstairs, wearing rain coats with hoods that covered our heads and tied tight with just a little open window to see out of. We were throwing balls across the mall, encouraging others with our actions. It was as if people knew what to do, everyone just started grabbing balls and throwing them at one another. There was screaming and the mall was loud and chaotic. So many balls were flying through the mall that it looked like a fight scene out of a Star Wars movie. Our prank was an absolute hit with our classmates, and for my crew it was priceless, and to this day, legendary.

The next day, Damian, Scooter, Chris and I were called separately into the office and questioned about the event. We couldn't understand how we had been singled out, because none of us had said a word to anyone else. We had promised one another early on that if any of us got caught, we would never sell out the others who did not. Ricky, the school principal tried her best to break us down and get us to do exactly that. We believed she was just going through a process of elimination and questioning us because we were obvious suspects. We eventually came to realize that the administration was just asking us questions to get the answers they already knew. Phil had sold us out. We were punished over the top for several reasons and mostly for the unfortunate timing of it all. Nicole Brown Simpson, a former student at our school, had been killed that week and this was a major news story because her ex-husband OJ Simpson was a suspect in her murder. We had not been aware, of course, that Inside Edition and other media crews would be visiting the school that day and meeting with the principal at the exact time our prank went down. I am sure Ricky felt more than a little embarrassed by the unruly behavior on her campus, and she probably disciplined us more harshly than she might have if the circumstances had been different.

We wanted to beat Phil up for selling us out! If not for him, the administration never would have been able to prove that we were responsible for the prank. Phil was ashamed and begged us for forgiveness. He was let out of any punishment himself in exchange for his confession to Ricky, but we all know damn well that living with his punishment of lost friendships was way worse for him back then and probably even now. The rest of us had to go around to all of the classrooms, preaching to the junior class about how it wasn't a smart idea to pull pranks because they would miss out on senior activities like we were. Phil was allowed to attend the senior events that the rest of us were banned from. He never even tried to join us in completing the chores we acquired as our penalty. The rest of us remained a solid team and fun as heck! We were together in the prank and together in the punishment as well. We did miss out on some senior events, but you can believe there isn't any senior activity I would rather have attended over the activities that we created ourselves and for the friendship we all shared. I have to believe that if Phil could go back in time and choose to stand by his choice and stand by his friends, to still be regarded and respected by us, he would. But, there are some mistakes you just can't fix. Going back to regain integrity is not an option. It's why striving for integrity and character together is such a tall order.

John became my hero that June when we were seated at graduation. The boys and I were separated and not allowed within a row of one another even if our last names coordinated us a seat together. Security guards conducted strip searches of us and other students before the ceremony because the administration was clearly afraid what stunt we might try to pull off. This was quite cool in our adolescent eyes and also simply hilarious. As Ricky was at the podium reminiscing on the year and imparting her final words of advice, a small plane flew into the airspace above the school. People were pretty focused on her speech until the plane's engine noise became louder and louder. When we looked up, we saw that a banner flowed behind the plane with the words: "RICKY, TENNIS BALLS FOREVER…" It was amazing! Damian and I looked at each other with our jaws open, and all the other students started cheering!

We couldn't believe it, and poor Ricky, with her tiny five-foot frame, just stared up in silence watching as the plane circled overhead again and again. It was an unforgettable moment! We later found out that the biggest prankster of all was John-with Diane's support for sure. He was stealthy about it and ever said a word to Damian or me about it, but we appreciated his gesture of support for sure.

The times I shared with those boys and other friends in high school and with Damian's family were highlights during a cloudy time in my life. I am grateful for my achievements in high school and also what I learned through my struggles during those formative high school years. I am beyond grateful for having found true friends to walk with. We were a handful, but a healthy one. We lived and weren't afraid to make mistakes and step outside the box. Our shared common interests and the competitive bouts between us led us to amazing experiences.

I missed my sisters very much during this time of my life, and I felt alone and alienated from my family after I chose to leave Kauai. I tried to call and connect with my sisters when I could, but it was difficult to maintain our relationship at a time when everyone shared the house phone, and long-distance calls were monitored closely. My dad would sometimes be able to track me down by phone, and would scream at me and call me names and then hang up on me. I did my best to shake it off and forget about him. I thought it might be about time to accept that he was probably never going to buy me the horse I had been begging for since I was a little girl! As much as I missed my family, I was never tempted, no matter how bad things were, to go back to Kauai. I was programmed for forward motion--no matter the roadblocks or fears I had to face.

My mom at this time was an hour or two away in Hemet. She was busy with her own life and working as a bartender. She would come to visit me sometimes, and I would occasionally drive out to visit her. But, she felt more like an acquaintance than a mom, and I felt like she tried to forget that mother side of her identity altogether after she lost us to my dad. I am grateful that we struggled to stay connected on some level, however distant, and that I kept the door open for the chance at a potential future with her.

When I was young and invincible, and living in a daily survival mode, I don't believe I sensed or experienced pain or suffering the way I now have as an adult. I think I was tougher then only because I honestly didn't know any better. My attitude has always been one of my best personal assets and has never allowed to let myself down or give up. I thank God for this--it has nothing to do with me. I always tell myself that when things get bad, be it emotional or physical pain, to keep moving and eventually I know that I will move through it. I know that everyone is different when it comes to handling adversity, stress, or trauma. For me, the answer has always been forward motion toward any hint of light at the end of a dark tunnel. It is all I knew then, and all I know today: Keep moving!

If I could sum up into one word what my high school experience really taught me, it would be APPRECI-ATION. Without my past hurdles and heartache during these formative years, I might not realize the deeper meaning of what it means to truly appreciate my current circumstances. Being able to appreciate the people and blessings in your life is liberating and has always propelled me to greater heights. I believe it is important that no matter where we are in life, that we are able to sit alone and appreciate the company we keep in our own skin. I can say with confidence that I have always tried to live my life with integrity and conviction. I may have felt inferior and unworthy of love from others at times, and doubted certain qualities in myself, but I took pride then and now in knowing that I lived life with passion and always with good intentions at heart.

    I will admit that I have many weaknesses just like everyone else. I have a mouth on me and I know that plenty of times my words and actions have hurt other people. I say bad words too much, and every year when everyone is making their New Year's resolutions, I decide to stop cussing and it lasts up until the moment I'm stuck in traffic on the 405 freeway. I know I am overly independent and that in itself has allowed many people to feel like I don't need them or can take or leave them. No one is perfect and I like to think of myself as a constant work in progress. As humans, we all know what we could be working on and I do try to always be working on those things. I used to be more defensive about my issues and now I just accept them and am grateful for the support and understanding from the people I love the most and for their patience for me as I grow and evolve.

    I know that I am reflected in every person that I choose to surround myself with in life. I can choose the people I engage with and most of all I can choose my attitude in any particular moment. Even when the world is caving in, I am always the only person in control of my own attitude. In high school, I learned the importance of surrounding myself with people of character who helped me be the best me possible. I have always had angels at my side, in human form, as well as the ones we can only feel. Even the animals in my life, have nurtured me and made me feel loved at times when I felt unlovable. Animals can reflect our own souls and energies, and I remember how replenished my heart felt when Fridge and Addy came into my life and took over the bed I slept in at Damian's house. I went to sleep at night feeling protected, safe, and loved, and that led me to have an even deeper compassion for and connection with animals forever after.

I have been blessed by many people and circumstances alike. Nevertheless, it took work and determination to get through certain situations in my life, and especially the instability of my high school years. But, I never gave up--and I never will! This God-given gift has kept me alive, fed me, clothed me, educated me, humbled me, and makes me feel like the most grateful individual in any room I have ever stood in and amongst any crowd. I feel rich and blessed beyond words. I fear that if I couldn't find any reason for gratitude and appreciation in every day, it might all be taken away in the blink of an eye.

Chapter Three

"LEAP OF FAITH"

After high school graduation, I was as determined as ever to just keep moving toward my simple goal of a happy and independent life--whatever that meant! I had always been openly obsessed with being a "famous female surfer," but I was more quietly yet equally obsessed with earning a college degree. I knew there would be a safety and security that would come along with a solid education. I had graduated with twelve varsity letters in four different sports and had even been recognized as the female California State Athlete of the Year my senior year. Paired with my solid GPA, these accomplishments should have ensured I was in high demand for plenty of colleges as a potential student athlete. I certainly wish someone within the coaching or administrative staffs at my high school could have taken the time or interest to pull me aside and insist I not let my potential go to waste. Instead, I seemed to slip through the cracks and when I look back I feel as if I sort of was allowed to disappear in plain sight. I can still vividly remember playing in the CIF All-Star softball game my senior year. My car was not working and I had taken a bus out to Diamond Bar and then walked a mile or so to get to the field. I arrived three hours early due to the bus schedule and my fear of arriving late for the game. I then found myself surrounded by these amazing female athletes from across the state and I suddenly became acutely aware of how different my reality was from all of the other girls on that field. Every player was announced during the opening ceremonies by her name and the college she would be playing for the following year. I was the single only player on that field to be introduced to the crowd as "Undeclared." I was later even named MVP of the game, and yet somehow I was the only girl out there who was "Undeclared" and with absolutely no scholarship in hand and no plan in place for college whatsoever.

  I actually had in fact been recruited by many colleges my senior year, but I kind of floundered and didn't know how to manage the travel requirements of visiting the various schools, the overwhelming requests that I provide personal footage, statistics, records, and so forth. I hadn't had anyone approach me with any guidance or a road map on how to prepare for all of this or even to simply help me respond to the recruiting letters. And of course I didn't ask anyone for help. I didn't realize at the time that the colleges themselves pick up the bill to bring you out to their campuses. As desperately as I wanted to attend college, I had not really had the chance to put in the legwork that was required when I was so busy just getting by each day during high school. I was barely managing to get by back then with what I had on my plate at any given moment, and I had ignored or thrown the recruiting letters away. When I graduated I had no solid plans for what would come next.

  I was still dating Kasey after high school and, like me, he had spent a lot of time between California and Hawaii. He did regular work with Surfing Magazine and I would hang out with him at their headquarters sometimes. You can imagine my surprise when the editor at the time, Nick Caroll, approached me one day with an offer to model for them! They wanted to do something very different for their yearly swimsuit pull-out spread. For the first time ever, they planned to use girls who *actually* surfed to model their bikinis--instead of just regular swimsuit models posing on the beach alongside surfboards. They chose Malia Jones (who was later named one of "People Magazine's 50

Most Beautiful People"), Ipo Mateo, and myself to be the models for the landmark issue. For the first time ever, Surfing Magazine was acknowledging powerful females in the sport of surfing, investing in female surfers, and recognizing them for their athleticism and not just as beautiful bodies in bikinis. I was beyond proud to know that I was one of the three lucky girls they wanted to have representing that revolution.

The magazine put us up on the North Shore of Oahu right in front of a fun surf spot in between Rocky Point and the world-famous Sunset Beach called Monster Mush. It was amazing! Here we were in a huge rented house, three of us young girls with our own stylist and make-up artist. We surfed and modeled every day while being photographed by the world-renowned Aaron Chang. We surfed all over the island and admittedly had all the attention of just about every other surfer each time we paddled out. We strutted to the beach with our slick little bikinis, sun-kissed skin, and sun-bleached hair. We felt fresh, feminine, and fierce!

This was the first time the mainstream surf world was seeing women portrayed as beautiful bodies paired with solid athleticism. Women's surfing at the time had a pretty stereotyped reputation that if you surfed, you were probably something of a tomboy. We were being showcased to demonstrate that girls could pull into barrels and ride hard with the boys, and then step out of the water into some slinky little dress and be just as feminine and respected that way just like anyone else. Our magazine spread sparked a trend in the surfing industry. Soon after, many of the surf companies began developing women's clothing lines, board shorts, swimwear, and more. Roxy took off with their more feminine ads of water-women. Women's surfing was now suddenly seen as "sexy," and the three of us had a lot of attention following the magazine release.

I began getting calls for jobs from respected companies like J-Crew, Elle Magazine, Shape Magazine and even Sports Illustrated. I was being called upon to do just about anything where the desired look was a combination of athletic, sexy, and feminine. Surfing Magazine called me one day and said that I should just get an agent since they were fielding so many calls from other companies interested in knowing more about us girls. Soon after that I got my first talent agent down in southern California.

As surreal as those circumstances might sound, my next opportunity came along in just about as unbelievable of a manner. In one of my eternal quests to stay busy and do things I was passionate about, I had organized a small beach clean-up back at home in California. When I was walking around with my black trash bag on the sand, a man approached me about potentially hosting a TV show. I told him that I had no experience at all, and that I was just a surfer who had done a little modeling. At the moment, I was even working as a part-time valet, parking cars in Laguna Beach. He said he saw potential in me, and invited me to meet him at a function at the Hard Rock Cafe in Newport Beach. Never one to walk away from interesting opportunity, I showed up that night. The producer quickly stuck a microphone in my hand and asked me to introduce the next band. I ended up doing some interviews on film later that night, and it was then and there that I began a career in television.

The same producers promptly asked me to host a show called "Planet X" that aired on Prime Sports--now known as the Fox Network. Each weekly episode would showcase alternative and extreme sports, complete with profiles of top athletes in their respective sports. I interviewed the athletes and then tested out the sport and participated alongside them as they shared their sport with the world. I worked intermittently on Planet X for about two years-covering segments from motorized surfboards and off-shore power boat racing, to dogfights in F-16 fighter jets. It was definitely extreme and also exactly what I needed to get my own fill of experience, travel, and adrenaline.

The seemingly endless opportunities that arose kept me plenty busy, and I didn't think much about any personal drama. I had my heart broken when Kasey slept with one of my best girlfriends, and of course I always felt that absence of my parents and the isolation from my sisters. I felt alone in some ways, but also very occupied with my job. I also felt loved by my production family--especially my cameraman, Jeff, who I believe to this day to be an actual saint. I look back and realize now what a handful I was for Jeff! He picked me up for work nearly every time we filmed an episode. We traveled together, ate together, and even when he wasn't working, I would call and pester Jeff with my emotional turmoil. He was always there. We were a good team and he had the patience to manage the wildly unamusing stunts that I would pull both on and off camera. I didn't know it then, but Jeff could see the pain and suffering I was going through deep inside. He was one of my only real friends at times and I leaned on him and trusted him with so much.

During that year or two after high school, I just kept busy with modeling jobs, Planet X, work with my surfing sponsors at trade shows, and traveling for surfing photo shoots. I split my time between California and Hawaii, spending most of the winter in Hawaii-excluding Kauai most of the time, in order to avoid my dad. Planet X was always a show I could fall back on and a platform for almost every job in entertainment I had thereafter. However, my job with Planet X could be dangerous at times; I was always risking my safety be it out in the water, riding futuristic watercraft machines with powerful engines, or doing crazy stunts in the air and on land. I didn't have the security of a family to fall back on if I somehow injured my face or body, so getting a college degree was a big part of my life plan. I worried that I was making the wrong choices at this point in my life when I should really be attending college. Even though I was finding success and happiness, the notion of a college degree was compelling because I knew that only I could earn it and that absolutely nobody else could ever take it away. I made the choice to forego my budding career in television and modeling in favor of the college experience.

Damian had decided to go to college at the University of Hawaii, Manoa, so I figured I would follow him there and I soon found myself walking on to the Wahine softball team as a freshman. I was paying for every dime of school and living expenses, and was busy trying to maintain work, academics, and the intense expectations of collegiate athletes. All this, plus trying to keep up with my obligations as a professional surfer. It was tough on me, and this time period is something of a blur. I do remember that at one point I lived with four strippers and my athletic department guidance counselor, and our household was never short on chaos. I came and went pretty quietly to and from work, surfing the North Shore and school. I still spent a lot of time pursuing my surfing and branching out to do some fitness modeling to save up money.

I had left behind a career in television and modeling, thinking I was pursuing a greater goal. However, I was not finding the experiences I had been looking for at the University of Hawaii. I had gotten injured right before the softball season started, and the coach decided to redshirt me which meant I could practice with the team but would not play any games that first year. I was working at Hard Rock Cafe in Waikiki parking cars and then driving a Pedi-cab until 2 am five days a week. I was so exhausted daily and felt like I wasn't learning anything in school anyway. I kept receiving calls from the producer of Planet X, as well as calls from various magazines and companies wanting to book me for photo shoots. It seemed that I was declining so many good offers in favor of college, but I was not finding college rewarding, meaningful, or even productive. Contemplating the decision to leave school and go back to the mainland was agonizing for me. I had never started anything I wouldn't finish--not since my first surf competition when my dad had dubbed me a Quitter. "College Dropout" sounded like just about the same thing in my head, and making the final decision to leave was hard on my heart. I reluctantly made this decision with much regret and sadness, but it was inevitably the right one for several reasons. Sometimes you have to let go to receive!

    I know now that walking away from something that isn't good for us makes us stronger, not weaker. I was so programmed to prove myself, to never quit, that I was making myself stay in a situation that wasn't serving me--just to prove to myself that I could get through it. When I came to that realization, I finally gave myself the permission to walk away. I won't lie; I still felt ashamed and like a Quitter indeed, but at least I ignored those thoughts and made the right choice for myself. For perhaps the first time in my life, I ignored my dad's voice in my head--and listened to my own heart and intuition instead. And so, I did it: I Quit. I was a College Dropout. And I was going to be okay.

Chapter Four

"DAUGHTER OF WESTWOOD"

"Things turn out best for the people who make the best of the way things turn out"
-John Wooden

What I am about to share when it comes to this next part of my life is nothing short of a miracle in my mind. I have shared this story with people a few times, and I still have to stop and gather my emotions. Even now, I am brought to tears as I think about the chain of events and the downright blessing I received when I chose to listen to my heart and return to the mainland. When I returned to California, I was welcomed back to Planet X and I took modeling jobs that included travel to New York, Miami, Puerto Rico, San Francisco, and Europe. I was somehow in demand, and this was good. The hectic pace took my mind off the regret and shame I felt for not having stayed in school. I still felt like a failure because of this, no matter how successful I might have appeared from the outside.

I had resumed shooting with Planet X, and Jeff called one day to let me know we were scheduled to do a segment for Reebok at the women's sports combine. These combines provide an opportunity for coaches and scouts to evaluate potential athletes for collegiate teams. We had already covered the the football combine with all of the top male football recruits about a month prior. I asked him what sports we would be covering that day so that I could gather appropriate gear. He said we were covering volleyball, basketball, and softball. I told him that I wouldn't play softball but that I'd be happy to do the other sports. I had a downright bitter feeling toward softball at that time; still harboring a broken heart after having been so close to my dream and goal and having left it back in Hawaii. As much as I had loved the sport and wanted it in my life, I also was mad and wanted to reject it and never play again! As always, Jeff was agreeable, and we headed to Los Angeles. When we got there, I was introduced to the women athletes before they were sent out to run through the drills in their respective sports. I remember the downright jealously I felt towards them. Here they were, in exactly the situation I had always dreamt of being in. These girls were on the brink of attending big-time colleges, many with full scholarships, and probably with supportive parents who would be cheering them on from the sidelines. I have always tried hard to be happy with what I have and not be jealous of anyone else. But I was still reeling from my failed college experience and was definitely envious at that moment of these other girls. Funny enough, I knew at the same time that they were all looking up to me, hoping to impress me, and hanging on my every word as if I were some celebrity.

There I was at the women's Reebok sports combine--taking place on the UCLA campus in the Westwood Village community of Los Angeles. After I spent some time talking with the athletes, Jeff and I geared up for the segments and got started. When I thought we were finished, Jeff said he wanted to head out to the softball field to do the last segment. I immediately refused; telling him that it was hard enough to be in that environment already, much less with all the softball recruits. I tried to refuse and then insisted I didn't have the proper gear. Unphased, Jeff pulled out my softball gear and bat bag with everything I would need. He reminded me that the UCLA Bruins were one of the best softball teams in the nation and it would be ridiculous to show up with footage for other sports and not softball. I knew he was right, but I still refused. I told him to go out and just get footage himself without me in it. He told me that we needed the interview with the coaches and at that moment, the UCLA assistant softball coach, Kelly Inouye, came walking past us. She asked if we were on our way out to the field to check out their combine. Jeff looked right at me and said, "Yes, we are just getting Danielle ready and then we will be right over." I was downright pissed off at Jeff, but now I had no choice but to gear up and get out on the field with the players.

I walked out to the field and spoke to Kelly about what and whom she would like us to profile, and what she would like me to do with the players. I ended up running the bases, hitting, and playing in the outfield. When we were done filming, Kelly asked me, "What's your story?" She specifically wanted to know my softball experience, age, and if I had any college eligibility. I told her that I had been injured and redshirted at the University of Hawaii, Manoa and that I still actually had four years of eligibility remaining. She asked me if I thought I might ever be interested in playing softball for the Bruins. She said that she would have the UCLA head coach Sue Enquist contact me to discuss the reality and possibility.

Walking back with Jeff to the van, I was speechless and can just remember my heart beating so fast that I could barely focus my eyes to see! When we reached the van, Jeff said, "See? You never know! What do you think, would you really ever come here and do this? You know this is the best team in the nation!" I remember sitting down on the side of the van, changing my shoes, and then just bursting into tears. I was sobbing into my hands so hard that I could barely breathe. I couldn't believe what was happening in that very moment. I could see the campus from where we were parked. It was amazing. It looks like a miniature version of a quaint European town with its beautiful red brick and even the infamous Pauley Pavilion basketball arena right in front of us. It was somewhere I never dreamed of being worthy of belonging to. I was overtaken with emotion and humbled at just the thought.

As Jeff and I drove home that day, I was choked up with a million "What if?" questions and wanting him to be able to give me all the answers. Jeff and I immediately began playing ball after our TV shoots, just playing catch and getting my arm back in shape. I already played regularly on the Killer Dana Surf Shop's softball team and I purchased a tee to practice hitting on my own time. One afternoon, Jeff was contacted by Sue Enquist, the Bruins head coach, in regard to my potential with the team. I spoke briefly to her as well but because of NCAA rules, we weren't permitted to meet in person. I learned that all of the teams' scholarships had been committed already, and that it would be a long shot to get me into school and on the team. It seemed insane the amount of paperwork I had to complete. I needed to retrieve records from high school and the University of Hawaii, of course, but then all the other roadblocks came up.

After much effort, I showed up to the softball office and athletic department proud to let them know that I had been cleared and would be joining them first thing in the fall when school would begin. I showed up the first day to pay my tuition that I had saved the exact amount for and when I arrived, the price for tuition had been tripled! The registrar said there had been a discrepancy with the dependent/independent comment on my registration form and that according to IRS, I was a dependent of my parents and not an independent as I had stated on my form. It also had me as an out-of-state transfer and not a California resident at that time. This would mean that I would need to pay out-of-state tuition. I cried so hard that I made the lady at the admissions office cry too. I tried to explain, but there was nothing they could do for me there or at that time. I plain and simply didn't have the funds to get in and support the annual tuition and living expenses as an out-of-state student. There was nothing I could do but to go back to the drawing board and prove that my dad was the one lying on his income tax forms when it came to me. The coach was pretty upset in general and upset for me as well. I wouldn't be allowed to step foot on the field that quarter and would be confined to the bleachers at best, so that's where I sat each day.

I didn't give up--not then and not ever! I went back over all of the checks that I had saved and chronologically organized in boxes. I had envelopes with receipts as proof of my independence. I had referral letters written by people who had housed me or helped me in one way or another, or just were willing to vow for me. My surf sponsors were supportive and pulled every check they had ever paid me from beginning to end. They were excited to have me able to represent them as a student athlete as well, and they were very encouraging during this difficult process. I created a report for the admissions board to review and also to double-check with the IRS if need be. I contacted the IRS as well, and told them that I had been independent of my parents for over three years at this point and had no contact whatsoever since I had left at age 16. I told them to ask my dad for receipts of his care for me, and proof that I was indeed a dependent of his. I covered as many bases as I could and tied off any potential loose ends that could block me from attending school the following quarter. I checked in with the admissions office nearly every day until I was given the answer that I so needed, deserved and wanted. YES! You are clear and you will be paying in-state tuition. Finally!

    I went through the process all over again, showing up to the athletic department this time with an exact amount and a smile. Everyone smiled for me, and that day, I became a UCLA BRUIN! I went proudly to the field ready to practice with a half-shirt and some short shorts on. Coach Sue told me that she never wanted to see me wear that again and that I had better cover up! It was classic. I was so accustomed to running around in bikinis and beachwear that I didn't even think about what I was wearing. I didn't make that mistake again! The girls checked me out pretty carefully and it took some time getting adjusted and fitting in late in the pre-season. Their softball team is highly recognized and I wasn't some big name softball recruit-which like they were accustomed to. They hadn't paid me too much attention when I had been watching practices quietly from afar. But, you prove yourself on the field first and foremost. Once you're in, you're in, but it doesn't happen overnight. I can't put into words how proud it made me feel to eventually truly belong to such an elite group--and especially to wear those four letters across my chest every day.

I had kept various cards, notes, and letters in a box that I carried with me everywhere I had moved over the past few years. After that first day of practice as a real UCLA Bruin, I went home and opened that scrap box. I sifted through the letters until I came to a card in the shape of a bear's face-a Bruin bear to be precise. Inside was a handwritten note from assistant coach Kelly Inouye, inviting me for a recruiting trip to see the school and team. It was the only recruiting letter I saved and simply because I liked the card. Amazing. I held it to my chest, and simply thanked God for this moment in my life and for the reality of this dream. I prayed that no one would ruin this opportunity or try to take it from me.

Playing college athletics at a Division-1 university is no joke. Your school and your team own you--whether you walk on or have a full-ride scholarship. When you step on the field, it's level and you fight for your position every day. Our softball team was a tight-knit family. Whether you loved the girl beside you or not, you stood for her, you cheered for her and you respected her for the same four letters she also wore across her chest. We were a team, a family, and I was never more proud than when I was amongst them. The girls were the best I had ever seen, so many big fish in one pond! Olympians and warriors--all of us working together and out to get the jugular of anyone who tried to step in our path or compete with us. It was what we did.

I personally believe there is no better coach to have walked on a field than Sue Enquist. She and I got along well and shared a love of surfing that I had yet to share with too many other women. We surfed together a few times and I was more than impressed at her ability and savvy in the water. She is an amazing woman and a tough badass when she wants to be. She is a Bruin through and through and she always stood firm on expecting us to maintain her standards. Standards to this day that have only contributed to me being my very best woman I can be.

All of us players have recounted our favorite Sue stories many times but one that stands at the top for each and every one of us is when we got in trouble for being referred to as "The Party Team." Sue came to us one afternoon and yelled so hard that she was spitting! She said she had been in the athletic department and some of the other coaches had made reference to her that we were the "hard partiers" and that their athletes had bragged about the fun parties that "the softball team" would have. That didn't sit very well with Sue and she made us believers real quick. It was raining that day and we were put out on the field, each few of us placed within arm's length of a championship banner. The outfield fence was blanketed with them. She began drilling us with up-downs and jumping jacks mixed with sprints in place. We did this until some, if not many of the girls were throwing up and a few even crying. She scared them! It was almost like BUDS training, she was yelling at us, "Quit if you don't like it! QUIT!" None of us did.

Those of us who didn't party were just taking it all in. Pretty livid, but at the same time, just taking it. That's what you do when you're a team. We were all beyond muddy when she finally called us to stop. We left the field silent that day, no cheers, no smiles, just silent and humbled. She knocked the spoiled right out of some of them. She said on our way out, "I had better not get one phone call from any of your parents in regards to this! If I do, so help you all!" It was hilarious. We didn't laugh that day, but we sure have laughed endlessly since. No one can truly appreciate the legitness of that lesson unless you experience it yourself or witnessed it. It was something else--and something that actually made us closer as a team and better for it. I am forever grateful to Sue for her kick-ass, technical, and strategic approach to coaching. Her legacy will live on through each and every one of us players and the Bruin spirit will always be a light for me no matter where in the world life takes me and no matter the storms I tread. I was grateful to have Sue in my life as someone who cared enough to make me dig deep and be my best. She took a chance on me when no one else did at this level. She believed in me and expected me to believe in myself. It was something a girl should probably learn from her mother, but Sue was more of a mother figure to me during that time of my life than my own mother had been.

  Anytime that I allowed myself to think about my own mom, I knew that her choices had hurt me in ways she never could see. I resented her sometimes for my pain, my suffering, my instability, and most of all for not being aware of my father's inappropriateness with me. I believe that she did drugs even more than before and she behaved even more irresponsibly than ever after she suffered the pain of losing both of her girls. I tried to stay minimally connected with her when I was living on my own, but it seemed that all I could do was watch her going nowhere-- and fast. I always believed I had the right to have a real mom, and I was angry at every wrong choice she made; choices that ultimately impacted Sadie and me just as much as her. Despite all of the excuses I might want to make for her now, there is no denying that she was very selfish and self-centered and she never put the interests of her daughters ahead of her own.

    My mom eventually ended up in jail; a place I believe can potentially change a person for either the better or worse. I am happy to say that my mom came out better for it, and I respect her tremendously for enduring such punishment, even though I was angry at the time. I remember when she first got out of jail, she was so worried about what I thought and if I loved her anymore. I was angry with her, but I also had so much compassion for some reason. She would call me on the phone and talk about wanting to give up and die. I felt helpless. I was trying my hardest to just be a normal college student. I wanted a classic and traditional collegiate experience, and UCLA was giving me exactly that. Yet, on nights when I would be tired from practice and needing to do my homework, my mom was still being selfish and putting herself ahead of me. I would spend four hours on the phone trying to console and reason with her sometimes, only to have her tell me that she was going to kill herself at the end of the conversation. It pained and exhausted me.

    I remember trying to tell my mom that she needed to stop worrying what anyone else thought and that she needed to do whatever it took to make herself happy and well. I reminded her what she had been through, that she had proven she could live through hard times, and that this in itself was a huge accomplishment. I told her that she needed to make herself proud first and then the rest of the of the world, including me would also be so proud. I didn't know how to love her then and I had to do it a bit rough at times. I was compassionate enough to give her the best I could, but underneath it all, I felt she was only finally coming around in my life to take from me. I felt that it was she who should have been adding to my life. Instead, I was caught in the position of fighting every day not to be a Taker myself, which made me resent my mom for taking from me and giving nothing in return. She was supposed to nurture and take care of me. She had never met my needs in that regard and yet she expected me to now provide that for her. My natural instinct to tend and befriend was simply missing here and I struggled.

    I felt unable to cope with my mom's problems and it finally became too much for me to handle. I eventually cut off contact with her altogether. She became really angry with me, but I didn't take it personally. I felt that she had already expected me to raise and mother myself, and now she needed me to mother her also! I couldn't handle that. I wanted my mom but I didn't even know what that meant. I couldn't understand her refusal to get up and keep moving forward. I to know adversity. You fight, you charge, and never give in or up. Neither of my parents possessed this perspective. As far back as I can remember, I had only seen things this way. For this perspective in life I am eternally grateful. However, I have since come to better understand that depression is a strong weapon that stands against human nature. There is no way to muscle it away; it takes technique and sometimes a gentle defense to muster enough strength to win that fight.

The Bruins fight song references the "Sons of Westwood" being "true" to the "blue and gold." However, I always took pride in thinking of myself as a true "Daughter of Westwood." UCLA gave me the chance to prove that I could be an amazing daughter--committed, hard working, and loyal--if given the respect, support, and compassion I had always craved in my environment. UCLA was a true home for me, a sanctuary even, that came complete with a true family. A home where I belonged and knew I deserved to be. And my softball teammates were sisters indeed at a time when I wished I could have my real sisters by my side.

      No matter how hard or taxing the work got in those years at UCLA, there wasn't a single day I didn't look around that campus and think, "Wow!" People sometimes say things like that, but I mean it with all my heart! UCLA is greatly respected for its academic and athletic programs alike. It was a genuine privilege to be there, and I took it all in. Every single day I gave thanks for being so blessed to be exactly where I was in life. I would frequent the libraries and just look around at the books, the architecture, and the people. I never could fully believe that I was part of it all. At the same time, I knew that I absolutely belonged there in every way. The UCLA campus is so beautiful, and for me it has an energy and a smell that if my eyes were closed and you took me there, I would know exactly where I was. UCLA will always be more than special in my heart. Anyone who knows me knows I am all about it! I get made fun of for being so passionate about my alma mater, and of course the rival USC haters love to instigate me. They are sure sorry when they do! I don't back down and I am never too shy to represent on any occasion.

My experience at UCLA will always serve as a moral compass. I am so appreciative of everyone and everything that made it possible for me to attend such an incredible school. I even had the privilege of meeting the legendary John Wooden in the training room, as well as many star athletes we see today in professional sports and the Olympics. I will probably never fully believe that I am part of such an elite group of women athletes whom I respect so much. I have seen so many of them succeed in many ways in life and know that we share a foundation of skill and strength that was honed in college under the discipline and direction of Sue Inquest and Kelly Inouye. I love all of my Bruin sisters and will never be far from my memories at that lovely UCLA campus. These people and experiences have all inspired me to want to be bigger than I ever believed I could be. I am grateful, inspired, and humbled.

I would sometimes drive down to Dana Point during college to see my Grandpa Sam and Judi and use their computer to work on school papers and projects. Grandpa Sam was so simple yet brilliant and he could always explain the most complicated things so they made sense. I remember one time, going over to his house to use the computer to write a paper for school. It was a history paper about some obscure Indian tribe. My Grandpa was asking me a lot of questions about it and when I gave vague answers, he kept digging. I was becoming a bit impatient with him and finally said, "Grandpa, it's lame! You don't know what I'm talking about, it's a paper on this indigenous Indian tribe called (whatever I said at the time…)." He immediately corrected me and said, "It's pronounced… (this or that) and their native chant is (this)!" I almost fell over! He then proceeded to tell me things about this particular tribe that was not even in the book. My professor was the one who wrote the book and so when he read my paper, he actually sought me out to ask where I had retrieved the tribal chant. I told him that my Grandpa Sam had told me about this tribe and the professor asked me who my Grandpa was and I just replied, "He's super smart." I was shocked that my grandpa knew more than my professor who had dedicated his career to the teachings and research of this particular tribe. I don't think I ever lost my patience with my Grandpa Sam again. I was humbled and even more in awe of him. I was put in place by his actions and knowledge, not his words.

When I graduated from UCLA with a Bachelor's degree in History, I invited my Grandpa Sam and Judi, John and Diane, and Damian to the ceremony. I was secretly saddened not to have my parents there. I was so proud of myself that day and disappointed that they weren't there to also be proud of me. I had people there who loved and supported me for sure, but nobody can replace the presence of parents at a significant moment in life like a college graduation. I didn't show it that day, but it hurt and embarrassed me not to have anyone there to represent my immediate family at such a proud, defining and wonderful moment in my life. I had maybe hoped deep down that Gini would have brought my sisters to see me graduate, or that my mom would have shown up--no matter the fact that our relationship was not in a good place at the time.

I was wandering around trying to find all the girls that were graduating from my softball team, when I found them in their caps and gowns, talking amongst themselves. I walked up and they turned to me with smiles but were pretty quiet. They circled me and Christie Ambrosi had a blue bag in her hand and approached me with it. Christie was my roomie for most of my career at UCLA and my best friend on the team. She and I laughed hard and often and we were always up to something interesting. I asked them, "What's up? What are you guys looking at me like that for?" They asked me if by chance my parents had shown up. I told them that they were not there, but that my grandparents and guardian parents were there. They all had their parents and relatives there, and they were just making sure I had support. Christie handed me a little blue Tiffany bag and said that they had all come together to buy me this gift.

The girls told me that one of the days when I was unable to show up at practice, some of my teammates had complained that it was unfair that I got to miss practice and still play in the games. Apparently, Sue promptly sat them down and exposed my situation to them. She explained to them that I paid for my school, my food, my living, and that they needed to stop judging or questioning anyone else's situation. She told them that they didn't know a tough time and also how lucky they were to have parents there supporting them and helping them financially and emotionally. I had never known of this talk she had with the girls. I always felt like I did so much to hide my reality--despite the fact that my parents were not present at even one single game. My teammates never treated me any differently for it--which I appreciate. I would have been truly embarrassed if I had known about this.

    I opened the blue bag and in it was a Tiffany, sterling silver ID bracelet with UCLA engraved on the front and my jersey number "13" on the back. It was unbelievable. I was beyond words and just began to cry. They all huddled around me, embracing me in a hug, crying with me. They said how proud they were and how much they loved me. They said how I inspired them and they called me their hero. It feels weird to write this and say something like that about myself because I'm nothing compared to any one of them. They were each my heroes that day, and to this day that moment we shared is one of the most powerful moments of my life.

We all headed into the auditorium after that and I sat there, staring down at the bracelet, looking around at everyone and everything around me. I looked up and waved at my family that was there, the smile on my Grandpa Sam's face and how proud he was for me. It was a moment in my life that time seemed to stand still. I didn't hear much of what anyone said during the ceremony. I looked around and found every one of the girls, my softball sisters that day who were also graduating. We were smiling at each other, relieved and proud and probably a bit taken back by it all. I wore my bracelet on one wrist and held the charm in my fingers, rubbing my thumb again and again across the UCLA letters. I wore it proudly, and to this day, it means so much to me. It's difficult to sit here and find the words to give justice to such an experience and also to such a powerful moment. To be noticed and loved and to be appreciated and accepted is something else. I felt like everything I had been through was worth it. During those college years, I had been given so much--but at the same time, I hadn't taken a thing from anyone. I felt worthy of gracing that campus and just plain worthy.

    I believe my college experience illustrates beautifully how important indirect opportunities can be in our lives.

If we do not think ourselves above or below anyone or anything, but acknowledge possibilities when they come, we keep ourselves open and able to receive the gifts of this universe. If I hadn't been walking around the beach collecting trash one day, I would not have been offered the chance to introduce the band at the Hard Rock Cafe. If I had not been willing to step outside of my comfort zone and take a microphone in my hand that same night, there would have been no TV hosting role with Planet X. And without Planet X, I certainly would not have been on the UCLA campus that fateful day of the combines when my life changed for the better. Rich or poor, I have never been too busy to stop and take a look or listen to what the universe sends my way. This is a gift that has never failed to continue to give back to me.

Chapter Five

"MAJOR LEAGUE MOM"

"There is no passion to be found playing small--in settling for a life that is less than the one you are capable of living"
-Nelson Mandela

When I graduated from UCLA in 2000, I was ready to devote absolutely everything to my career. As tends to happen in life, as soon as I graduated, the opportunities I was finally ready to take full advantage of seemed to suddenly disappear. I remember that first year after graduation being pretty tough in terms of getting work. I tried to spread myself out in order to maximize any opportunity as well as to just survive those dry times. It was so ironic to find myself in that position, given that as far back as I could remember I had struggled to balance school and sports and work. It always seemed like the busier I had been in college, the more job offers would come in faster than I could take them.

Various modeling, surfing, and television hosting jobs had fed me and paid for my education those past four years of college. But, there had been plenty of times when incredible opportunities came along that I had to refuse because of school and softball. There is one such job in particular that comes to mind. I had gone into the casting office at least five times for a potential hosting position with a show at E! Entertainment during my senior year. The field had been narrowed down to just a couple girls from hundreds of auditions. It seemed like an amazing opportunity. The main producer pulled me aside one day before casting and told me that I was a favorite and his particular pick, but that I would need to leave UCLA if I wanted the job. I was a senior at this time and my softball career was finished. I couldn't understand why it was so pertinent to them that I drop out of school. I had done that once in Hawaii and I absolutely would not do that again.

I told the producer that I would balance all of my responsibilities and that the show would be my first priority. If I needed to travel for the show, I assured him that it would never pose a problem. He told me that my decision was critical to their decision, and that I would need to let them know that week if leaving school was something I would commit to doing for the job. When I returned for the final read and audition, that same producer asked me what I had decided. I told him that I would not agree to leave school in order to get the job. It was a gut decision and easy for the most part. In theory, there was really no reason that I should have had to quit school. I felt this situation was more of a control issue for them, wanting to be sure the talent they chose would be submissive to their demands. I knew I was capable of balancing everything and that I would have earned my degree in mere months. I was not going to get so close to accomplishing such an enormous personal goal and then give it up just to be on TV. This was, though, admittedly a really huge project that I lost out on. I have watched the host that got the job launch her career off of that role and become a household name. In my heart, I made the right decision and if I had to go back and make that choice all over again, I would not change a thing. Life throws us many moments where these decisions are made that set us on certain paths on our life journey. No matter how firm I am in knowing that I made the best choice for myself, I can only wonder sometimes where that particular role might have taken me in life. I sacrificed for my degree and it definitely hurt my career. The entertainment industry is tough at times when it comes to peer pressure and influence. It pays to be strong as far as your character and mental stability go, but it can sure cost you on the outside with respect to where your career goes. I can recall plenty of times and situations where I might have gotten further in the industry or into higher positions by compromising myself or my integrity, but I would have sunk to a lower position as a person. I am proud of my career and the choices I have made. I never compromised my morals or self-respect for jobs or opportunities. I stood strong and worked hard to be my best for every job I got and for every project I worked on. I took a lot of pride in every position, and tried to maximize what I gave to each and every client.

    I have always refused to compromise my priorities or principles, but at the same time I have never been too proud to do what it takes to prove I deserve an opportunity that I want. I had one particular audition for a commercial that comes to mind that was scheduled at the Rose Bowl swimming pool in Pasadena. I knew that some diving was required and I thought I could manage a basic dive well enough to get through an audition. I was rushed for time and showed up toward the end of the casting call. When I walked onto the pool deck, there was a production team in place with cameras and the other divers were already wrapping up as I checked in. These other ladies looked like Olympic caliber divers to me! I back-stepped straight off the pool deck and called my agent immediately. I told him that I don't dive at their level and that I was going to leave. My agent told me to just go in there and do what I could.

    I was so nervous walking up to the diving board. I approached and could tell immediately that the director and even producer really liked me and were very interested. It seemed that I looked the part they wanted, so I just know that they weren't expecting me to do what I did next. When I stepped onto the diving board, it was really springy so I walked up a bit to adjust it. I didn't realize that I had just made it even more springy! When I went to dive, the board sprung me up so high into the air and I over-rotated onto my back and slapped the water. Hard. I was so embarrassed that I didn't even want to come up for air. When I did finally resurface, I said out loud, "I'm just a little rusty…I'll go again." I could see the disappointment on the director's face. Well, I approached the board and proceeded to do the exact same thing again on my second attempt! I was so embarrassed, but I was mostly upset to miss out on this potential opportunity for the commercial. I knew they had initially favored my look for the part, and it frustrated me to know that my poor execution of a simple dive was going to lose the job for me. I could tell the producer and director were almost as disappointed as I was with my awful performance.

I decided to walk straight up to the director and ask him what kind of dive they were going to use in the commercial. He told me it was a swan dive and that he was disappointed that I couldn't do it because I had the exact look they were searching for. I told him that I was just "rusty" and hadn't dove in a long time. I told him that if he would give me one week that I would master the best swan dive imaginable. He actually agreed to give me a chance! The next afternoon, I went to the pool deck at UCLA and marched up to the UCLA head diving coach. I told him I simply needed to learn a swan dive and that I would pay him to teach me. He said he couldn't accept money to teach me anything, so I told him I would buy him and his girlfriend or wife dinner anywhere he wanted in LA. He finally agreed and told me to just join in with the women's dive team at practice. I spent hours diving and practicing in that pool with the team and on my own every day for the next week. And when the week was up, the director really did come out and watch me dive again for himself. He couldn't believe it when he saw my perfect swan dive! He gave me the job on the spot and that 5-meter swan dive earned me a Cannon commercial that paid the equivalent of my last two quarters of tuition and room and board at UCLA. Worth the effort!

I know I have been blessed by many of the circumstances and opportunities that have come my way, but when I create a goal for myself I pursue it whole-heartedly. The entertainment and sports industries are similar in many ways. Being an athlete first and foremost gave me the strength to push forward and the confidence not to take criticism in my modeling or acting work too personally. I have tried to always look at my clients as being my "coaches" for the job, and that perspective allowed me to approach each job simply focused on the goal of getting it done right. I have seen amazingly beautiful girls turn into insecure wrecks because they take it personally when they are treated harshly during shooting or even the audition process. Most models and actresses hear "no" exponentially more often than "yes"--and we have to develop thick skin if we want to survive each job and live to see the next paycheck. It's similar to the statistics in baseball…if you fail 7 out of

10 times at bat, you just might be an All-Star! Even the most successful of models and actresses have more rejections than successes. What matters most is how we handle ourselves when people or circumstances are telling us we don't deserve something.

By keeping my eyes wide open and being open to considering anything, I ended up being connected through a friend to an incredibly successful businessman named Frank who was questioning the loyalty of people in his circle. He didn't have anyone he trusted, and my friend had told him he could count on me to be capable as well as loyal in anything he needed. Frank asked me if I would be interested in working with him in NYC and I agreed. And so, just like that, I was back and forth from LA to NYC--certainly intimidated and unsure of what I was doing, but eager to capitalize on this opportunity to explore the high-powered corporate world. Frank gave me confidence by trusting me in a position of making big decisions for both him and his business. I watched everything and everyone around him and reported back to him. He taught me everything I needed know about the business world. I looked out for him, and he looked out for me as well. He taught me that being financially independent and savvy in business was important because it would give me the freedom to fall in love someday for the right reasons instead of getting stuck with a man just for stability. I took that wisdom to heart.

    I was in New York only a few short weeks after the devastation of the terrorist attacks on 9/11. I walked to Ground Zero, and just being there so close in space and time to the event was a life-changing experience. I saw the chain-link fence around the area with all the pictures of missing people, and my heart fell into my stomach. I silently looked at all the pictures of those people, and thought about the families or loved ones that had hung these on the fence in the first place. I couldn't believe the rubble and mess and that there were still people missing in the pile of collapsed concrete and metal. I had such awful, angry emotions brewing in my chest. I felt so mad and downright aggressive. I felt such intense hatred toward the people who did this to our nation, and could not even begin to wrap my head around something of this magnitude. It was one thing to watch the two twin towers fall to the ground on TV and to hear about it over the news, but a completely different experience being there, smelling the stench of dead bodies and burnt cement and metal, taking it all in in person. It was painful, but something as an American that I needed to take in and experience firsthand.

The experience and the work and income I had in NYC took the pressure off my financial situation and once that happened, of course more entertainment work started to trickle back into my life. I booked a job for Speedvision called "Pro-Truck TV," with a hosting position with Ivan "Ironman" Stewart. It was an off-road show, covering Baja 500, Baja 2000, desert racing through Nevada and so forth. The Pro truck class was a driver's class amongst all the races and Ivan's personal creation. This was a very outdoorsy job--complete with wind, dust, and lots of awesome and literally "driven" people.

Ivan Stewart is a veteran of the sport and reminds me of John Wayne. He was tall, robust, in great shape and very witty. He is emblematic of the sport of off-road racing and helped create TRD (Toyota Racing Development) for Toyota. I remember my first day meeting Ivan and all the drivers. I was asked to report to Barstow, California, for filming. I arrived that morning with my producer and director and in my endless attempt to make people laugh, I thought it might be funny to throw in a pair of false buckteeth for my introduction. As you can imagine, anyone who puts these teeth in takes on a look all their own--and it isn't necessarily a desirable one! Ivan played it pretty cool when he met me, but he definitely wasn't expecting the host of his signature show to have big buckteeth! He greeted me warmly, but couldn't help also laughing right in my face. Little did I know that the camera was already rolling at the time of our introduction, and they ended up turning the joke around on me--airing my ridiculous grin right on national television. Ivan and I had a great time that year and did a good job together. He is an amazing person with a lively spirit and a big heart, and I also loved spending time with his son, Brian Stewart, and his granddaughter, Chancy.

    I met a lot of wonderful people during the shooting of that show and was taken aback at the passion these people demonstrated for their sport. It's dangerous, exciting, and definitely expensive and with very little reward as far as prizes or money goes. The show taught me that professional sports aren't always about winning medals or money at the finish line. Because of that, I found it even more compelling to partner with and learn from so many of these passionate people along the way. These people were in it for the joy of the journey in just getting there. That was something that I took away from my experience in the Pro-Truck world, at least.

After the show wrapped, I continued to host other shows with NBC, Fox Sports, and I did other work with varied networks and magazines. I was keeping busy working, surfing, dating a little, and just enjoying life in L.A. with friends. My best friend Courtenay and I were always up to something fun as well. It was during this time in my life that I met Mark at a BBQ in the home of a mutual friend. I was actually on a date with someone else that I played baseball with. He wanted to leave early to head up to a different party in the Hollywood Hills and I didn't want to go. He left. I stayed. And that was another decision that would change the path of my life forever, I guess!

Mark approached me that evening and we just instantly clicked and talked for the rest of the night. He asked me out on a date for the following night. Our baseball team played right in Beverly Hills and I loved it and would never miss a game. I remember telling Mark that I couldn't go out the next night because I had a game and couldn't miss. He told me that he also had a baseball game that he couldn't miss. At this point, I was assuming that he also must have played baseball in the same type of league as me and that we could probably get together the following night. When he told me he had another game the day after, I wondered what league he played in that had more than one game per week. He invited me to just come to his game and we planned to go out after. We were planning to see the movie, *"Pearl Harbor."* He gave me directions to the game and said he would leave tickets for my friend Courtenay and me. At this point, I was thinking, "Tickets…multiple games per week…What league is this and what team is he on? The National League of MLB baseball is what league, and the Los Angeles Dodgers is what team!

    Courtenay and I arrived at Dodger Stadium in L.A. and found ourselves seated in the very front row where the whole team could see us as we walked to our seats. I remember Mark waving to me from the dugout, and I am certain my face turned red. I remember being totally nervous and somewhat embarrassed sitting in those seats. Mark had obviously told his teammates that he had a date, and many of them seemed to keep looking our way. I am sure they were giving Mark a hard time and just doing whatever else the players do to heckle one another in these circumstances. When Mark first came out of the dugout to bat, he went to warm up in the on-deck circle which was directly in front of our seats. With the bat in his hand, he waved to me with his pinky finger and from then on, for years, that was our wave.

Mark is very handsome by most standards, and he seemed to be a fan favorite when he played with the Dodgers. I fear that I probably made some enemies of more than a few women at the stadium that afternoon when he waved at me! I was so embarrassed, and even more so when I had to wait for him at the bar afterwards. Mark had asked that I get a ride with Courtenay to the game so that he could drive me himself from the stadium later. When the game ended, I sat at the bar on a stool and there were people working in the dugout club ushering people to move out and clear the area. I was asked to leave, and I had to say that I was waiting for one of the players. The usher asked, "What's his name?" I looked at the guy and quietly said, "Mark." He then asked, "What's his last name?" I sat there for a minute, remembering all the letters that had taken up his jersey on the back, nearly dragging on the grass behind him and I grinned and said, "His last name starts with a G but that's all know." He laughed politely and told me I could wait where I was. It would be a long time before I could pronounce, much less spell, the last name

Grudzielanek! I felt like such a cheeseball. I am sure there were women waiting for these guys every day--and many of them.

When Mark came out of the locker room, he was cleanly shaven and nicely dressed. He was incredibly polite, gentle-mannered, and very sweet. He apologized for the game going into extra innings as if it was his fault. I laughed and said it was fun to watch and thanked him for the amazing tickets. We walked to his car, where he opened my door and even started to help me with my seatbelt. He was over the top sweet! We were headed to see Pearl Harbor, but when we got to the theater we found that tickets were sold out even through the next night. We settled for dinner at a steakhouse, followed by a couple games of pool. Mark is something of a pool shark, so today he tries to claim that he "let" me win the first game or two--but I know better. I remember us talking about everything under the sun and him seemingly paying me compliments on the hour. He was so down-to-earth and fun. He asked me out for the very next night even before the date had come to an end.

We dated this way for a few months, and it started to seem like we were getting pretty serious. He was always so sweet to me, but when I began to truly reciprocate his feelings, he started backing away. This behavior confused and hurt me. We took some time from each other and one evening I received a call from him and we began dating again. We talked back and forth about the whole thing, why it had ended and why we were so inclined to rekindle. There is a lot of fear that people have to deal with when engaging in relationships. Feelings start brewing and as good as it may seem, it can bring up a lot of not so good things from the past. It's important to face these things before you decide to move on into relations with others, because other people don't always deserve to sift through your trash with you. Every relationship has its own issues, and bringing the past with you into any new relationship can be disastrous.

  Besides the past having its own influence in Mark and my relationship, his family played their own significant negative role. I know it's not unique to our situation, but some things are only magnified in a relationship where one of the people is famous or makes an exorbitant amount of money. Mark was doing well with the Dodgers and in baseball in general. But, I also was now making great money--not millions a year, but great for a single 24-year-old--

and I was absolutely not looking for anyone to take care of me. I believe Mark's brothers had something that many families of professional athletes have and that's called a sense of entitlement. They took anything they could from him and on top of that they never took even five minutes to get to know me or give me a chance. They assumed that I was some L.A. gold-digger trying to hitch onto Mark for a paycheck. It's how they treated me and when I finally asked them why they "hated" me so much, they simply said "You aren't our kind of people!"

    No matter how they treated me, I did things like pick them up from the airport, used my own money to fill Mark's fridge when they came to town, and made sure they had rides to the game in the evenings after Mark had already gone to the field. It didn't matter how kindly I treated them, they were nasty, rude and would even move and sit away from me at the games. I could go on and on, filling these pages with details of their antics, but I won't. I call people like this low-class, desperate, and insecure. I never could understand how they couldn't just be happy for their own brother. Mark loved me and I loved Mark with everything I had. I did my best to be distant but kind to them and endure their treatment of me.

Even without added family stressors, life in MLB baseball is tough on any relationship. These players are on the road and playing games for eight months of the year. I was always comfortable with Mark, and I never worried or felt like we would experience a lot of the same challenges that many high-profile couples do. It is an obvious stereotype for any professional athlete, and one of the first things people would ask me about or warn me about when I first began dating Mark. We both traveled for work and were surrounded by plenty of potential temptations, but the trust between us seemed to come naturally and easily. I never questioned him and he never questioned me. I was in love with Mark and we seemed to both be too content together and busy to worry about other people at all. We supported each other's work and careers and I was his training partner when it came time to get ready for the season. We would run together, play catch together and I would play wherever he needed me to on the field to help him practice or throw balls in the infield. I even pitched a lot of his batting practice. I loved watching him play, and appreciated so much that he would include me with his preparation and routines.

I continued to keep busy with my own career and took on work when I could in Florida where Mark had another home. I was booked nearly daily with various jobs, my day rate being between $5,000-$15,000 a day. I was all over the country and loving life. In 2002, I had a modeling shoot not far from Mark's house in West Palm Beach. I was feeling beyond bloated--and when modeling sports bras, tiny shorts, and bikinis, this just wasn't acceptable! Talk about pressure! And I'm not just talking about the pressure of the bloating on my bladder. I had taken water pills to try to alleviate the bloating, and gas pills as well. Nothing would work. The photographer had his insecure fiancé working as a stylist on the set, and the two of them wouldn't stop arguing over the fact that she thought he was "looking" at the models! Of course he was looking at us! He had to look at us through the lens in order to take pictures, right? It was just a nightmare shoot to begin with and I was being asked repeatedly to "Please suck it in if you can…" Yep, they will say exactly that if they have to or even want to. I don't blame them. I looked like I had swallowed a small volleyball. I was miserable, irritable, and ready to be done with the drama couple. Mark was finishing up his season and he had asked me to stay for a while with him in Florida. The client had asked me if I could stay another few days, but I said I couldn't stay and I left at the first opportunity. By the time Mark came to pick me up, I was waiting out on the street corner with my suitcase, beyond ready to go. He laughed when he saw me and I asked him to please just get me out of there!

I was feeling a bit anxious as to why I was feeling so many unusual symptoms of irritability and bloating. When you model body-aware stuff like sportswear or swimwear, you get good at knowing what to eat the night before, as well as what not to eat or drink, in order to be camera-ready and professional when it comes time. I had never had such a problem like this before. I asked Mark if he wouldn't mind stopping at the store on the way to the house. I hopped out of his car and went straight to the aisle where they sell tampons and pregnancy tests. I always find it funny how they put the two of these together, sometimes side by side! I picked up the pregnancy test and looked at the tampons as if they were looking back at me with a little smirk like "Ha ha, not today honey!" I had to go buy a snack so that Mark wouldn't notice that I had gone in to buy a pregnancy test.

When we got to Mark's house, he went to unpack his things and I went straight into one of the guest bathrooms. I opened the test up and peed on the little stick as fast as possible. I don't think I was even done peeing before the second line started to come into vision. I don't remember what test I took, but it was the one where if there is only one line then it's negative and two lines it's positive. It was positive before I could actually set it down and wash my hands! The package comes with two tests and it says to take the tests in the morning as opposed to afternoon. It says that the tests are a bit more accurate in the morning. Whatever. I took the second one right then and there! Positive! "No! I'm a model, damnit, I can't get fat!" This is what was going through my head as I sat there on the toilet in complete disbelief!

I immediately called Courtenay and told her my news. I don't even think I was off the toilet. I was sitting there with two positive tests, and positively freaking out! I had just about signed a contract with Fox Sports and was on my way to the major leagues of my own career and now I was pregnant! I was 26, not married, and pregnant! Courtenay was calm as she always is and she got me to calm down also. She asked me if I had told Mark yet, and I told her I was still sitting on the toilet in his guest bathroom! I kept saying, "I just can't be pregnant right now! This totally messes up all my stuff!" I was so selfish!

Courtenay said that Mark and I would be good parents and that I should talk to Mark right away.

That afternoon, I was eating like a bottomless pit and downright pig! We were in the kitchen and I finally found it in me to tell Mark that when I had gone to the store, I had bought a pregnancy test. He looked right at me and said "Well?" I told him that the test was positive. Twice. He was beyond excited and told me that we were going to be awesome parents and that he was very happy. He said he felt like I wasn't as happy about it and that I was kind of wrecking the moment. I tried to explain to him that my whole life was about to change and that everything I had worked so hard for in my career was a waste. He kept reassuring me that none of it would change and that in the off-season, he would take over with the baby at home so I could focus on my work. I remember specifically him saying what a great team we would make and that he would be sure to support me in my career in the off-season. I was on board, and it wasn't two days later that we were engaged. He told me that he had an engagement planned all along and that all his teammates had known about it. It made me feel a little bad--as well as more than a little suspicious--to be getting engaged only days after he found out I was pregnant. He assured me it was already something he had wanted to do.

I got a call from my agents telling me that I had booked the cover of Sports Illustrated for women and I was ecstatic! Then I remembered I was pregnant and most likely it wouldn't happen. I told the agents and they told me to show up anyways and leave it up to the magazine if they wanted to use me or not. I wasn't showing in a way that anyone would notice I was pregnant but I also wasn't my lean self and I would have thought it not a possibility. When I showed up and told them, they could care less and proceeded with the shoot as if I wasn't pregnant at all. By the time the cover came out, I was very pregnant and glad I had done it.

As that fall turned into winter, I began to show and was lucky to not experience too much morning sickness. I mostly got carsick but I didn't really throw up too much. I knew from the beginning that pregnancy wasn't for me-- and that all the things I had heard about it being so wonderful were nothing short of blatant lies! We had just purchased and settled into a house in the Cheviot Hills of Los Angeles, right near the Fox studios when two weeks later, Mark was traded from the Dodgers to the Chicago Cubs.

Even though he wouldn't leave Los Angeles until February, it was going to be hard on us--and me in particular with my due date that June of '03. The only good thing about the trade was that he would be in Arizona instead of Florida for spring training, so he would only be an hour away by plane.

    I found that living alone in LA and not being able to work in my own career made me miserable. I felt left out. I couldn't play baseball, couldn't surf, wasn't getting my regular modeling and acting work, and I didn't feel comfortable calling up my usual friends since they were all about the activities I just mentioned. I did establish a routine of swimming at the outdoor aquatic center on Olympic Blvd. That was my only regular activity and chance for "fun" each day--swimming 30 laps and enjoying knowing that I was making the lifeguards nervous that they would possibly need to deliver a baby on the pool deck!

    I experienced some pregnancy complications and needed to have an amniocentesis. I was reassured that everything was okay, but I was worried and alone. I felt alone when Mark was away and alone when he was home in L.A. I was lonely and depressed, and the further along I got into pregnancy, the further Mark and I drifted apart. One day, I woke up and realized that a mysterious pillow was sleeping in between us and that we hadn't shared any kind of affection in months. I am an affectionate person and this hurt me deeply and probably played on the sense of depression I was already feeling. I asked Mark one day about the pillow and he played dumb. I told him that he hadn't even hugged me in weeks and definitely hadn't kissed or tried to be more intimate with me. He began to tell me that he wasn't attracted to the way I looked as my belly grew and that it made him feel weird at the thought of us being intimate while I was pregnant. I was really upset to hear this and deeply hurt. He pulled away from me even more, and we started fighting pretty bad to the point where we wouldn't even talk for weeks at a time.

Mark was at spring training in Arizona in February and March, and then off to Chicago for opening day in 2003. I only saw him one time that spring in San Francisco before I would see him again at the hospital hours before Bryce was born that June. We fought horribly and I had never felt more alone or insecure in my life. I am certain that chemicals played a part in my feelings as well as mood, but I didn't have the support of my partner and felt as though he hadn't maintained his part in our so-called "partnership." I was heading toward such a great unknown and I felt lonely and completely unsure of anything and everything. For perhaps the first time in my life, though, I couldn't just follow my own ambition and pursue what made me happy. I was in charge of another vulnerable and innocent life now, and that knowledge kept me focused on putting our baby first no matter how that impacted me as a person. I got up each day and ate well, swam, and tried to be relaxed and positive. I was honestly miserable much of the time, but I did what anyone would do…it's called being a Mom!

I remember sitting on the couch at our house in L.A. on opening day for the Chicago Cubs in 2003. I had been watching the MLB channel to see if there was even going to be a game due to snow. While it was 85 degrees in Los Angeles that day, it was only 22 degrees in the Windy City. The Dodgers were getting on with their opening day in short sleeves while the Cubs had head socks on and possibly the only and first time I had ever seen Mark in sleeves under his uniform. It was surreal to see these guys on the field and the stands still sold out to capacity with people in head-to-toe winter wear. The maintenance crew had plowed the field twice that morning and there was still snow and frozen ivy covering the outfield fence. I remember thinking to myself, "There is no way I'm going to be able to handle that!" Little did I know at that point what being a Cubs fan is all about!

I was similarly sitting in bed watching the Cubs game one afternoon that June, when Sammy Sosa was up to bat and he hit a ball that sent his bat spinning through the infield in a strange way. As I saw the umpires on the field huddle around his bat and inspect it, my contractions grew and I felt as though I had wet myself! I knew what they were about to report on the TV but I seriously couldn't believe it. Mark had been on third base when Sammy came up and he had safely crossed home plate when Sammy got his hit. Mark was well into the dugout when they ejected Sammy out of the game for having a suspected corked bat and they sent Mark back to third base. It was all over the sports channels and the news stations. Mark was pissed to have to go back to third and the manager, Dusty Baker, looked mortified but kept his cool and continued with the game.

In the meantime, as I watched Mark and the drama unfolding on TV, I was sitting in bed with a slow leak of water from my uterus and making calls to the doctor's office letting them know my status. I had seen the mucus plug about an hour before in the toilet and that day in particular had been tough to finish my regular 30 laps in the pool. The contractions were heavy and frequent during my swim and I would have to stop mid-lap until each contraction finished.

I had developed a friendship with my doctor, Debbie Krakow, and I called her to let her know what was going on. She told me not to stress too much but to get to the hospital in due time. I didn't want to rush to the hospital and be there any longer than necessary. As I drove to the hospital in Mark's Hummer, I kept having to pull over to the side of the road to labor through contractions--they were so incredibly painful. When I made it to the labor and delivery area, the nurses put me straight into a wheelchair and got me up to the room I would labor in for the next 28 hours.

I was already feeling so alone, and by this time I was also incredibly mad at Mark. We hadn't spoken in nearly two weeks, and it was only a matter of a day before my due date. I tried calling him on the way to the hospital to let him know I was in labor but his phone was off. I was incredibly pissed! Thank goodness I had my friend and Mark's teammate, Eric Karros', number. I called him for help in getting hold of Mark. He happened to be out with Mark at the time and he promptly handed him the phone. I told him I was in labor and asked why wasn't his phone on? I was pissed and yelling at Mark and he hung up on me. I called Eric's phone back and Mark answered, yelling back at me and then he hung up again. When I called back a third time, Eric answered and did his best to be neutral and calm us both down. I told him that I was in labor and on my way to the hospital and that Mark had better change his attitude if he wanted to be allowed in my room! I was seriously beyond angry! I received a call about three to four hours later from Mark telling me that he was getting a flight and would be at the hospital around 8 the next morning. He hoped that I would be able to wait until then to give birth.

I had a corner room at the hospital, with plenty of space and with windows that looked out over Beverly Hills. Dr. Krakow had called ahead to have them make room for me in a nice room that was private. She took such good care of me during and even after my pregnancy. Even after the baby was born, she would drop by to visit me and bring me food at home. That evening, I lay in the hospital bed, hooked up to just about everything I could be connected to in the room. The nurse had asked me three times if I was ready for the epidural and I had answered her the same every time. "No thank you, I won't be getting one of those." She replied each time with, "You'll be begging me for one soon." I assure you that I never begged her for anything!

5/07/03

Well, I'm nine months tomorrow and it's finally hitting me that you are real and that my life is about to change forever. I realize that there will never be anything else like you that will come into my life and touch it, light it up that way you will. I am so excited for your healthy, safe arrival. It is a bit scary as well, the whole process and all, but I feel as though I have done my best as far as preparation and the rest is in God's hands. I have the most amazing pictures of you that have been taken over the last few months. The ones taken last week are absolutely mind-boggling. I can't believe that you are here inside me, kicking, turning, and pushing all over. Your lips are so beautiful and truly captivating. I have this feeling that you will look like your Daddy.

The monitors were beeping every few minutes and I tried my best to rest, but I just couldn't. I had Mark on my mind, and of course the safe arrival and health of our baby and even my own health. I had no idea what to expect, other than knowing I was probably going to be in a hundred times more pain then I already was. I was alone in the room lit by the monitors displaying the typical green and red lights with the accompanying blinks and beeps. The bathroom light was on and the light splayed across the room like a white four by four coming out of the concrete wall and onto the dark floor. It was cold and I felt lonely. I felt a little scared, but excited at the same time. I wished that Mark was there with me and more so, that we were doing this together and happily.

6/04/03

Hey there little stinker! Well our day to meet has finally arrived and I have been here in the hospital listening to your heartbeat for the last 10 hours. We have quite a journey ahead of us and I am so excited to meet and see you. Your Daddy is on his way as well. Everyone is calling to greet you and things are a little overwhelming. I will see you soon as you cross over from your little heaven and into the world. God bless and may the Lord watch over us and recover us from this long journey.

Mark got into town and to my hospital room the first thing the next morning and it was only then that I allowed the nurses to start my pitocin. Boy does that drug rock some contractions! I was toughing it out at this point, and nurse kept offering me an epidural. I was deathly afraid of being a paraplegic and I wasn't willing to risk that or any other potential side effects of the drug. I had already mentally prepared myself for the worst and knew that fighting it would be stupid and only make it all worse. After all, when you think about it, the baby *is* coming out whether you are hurting or not! I was ready to take the pain no matter what and knew my baby's safe arrival would be my reward.

As difficult as laboring was, to be honest, being pregnant at all really just wasn't my thing. I will be honest in saying that I disliked it every step of the way. I believed all happily pregnant women to be liars! No one had told me the truths about this process. To me, there was nothing nice about it except for the end result. Pregnancy was hard on my body, my mind, my chemical make-up, and just everything. It was even hard on my relationship. Women are tough and I respect every woman who has given birth! As awful as the pregnancy itself was on me, the birthing process was scarier and much worse.

When I was in the 18th hour of labor, Dr. Krakow came into the room and talked to me seriously about taking the epidural. I wasn't happy about this and wasn't at all on board. The anesthesiologist happened to be from Kauai and he was also in the room trying to talk me through the process, telling me how rare paralysis actually is in patients. I said I was fine, but Dr. Krakow wanted me to have the shot. She said that I was only dilated to 4 and that I wouldn't have the energy to deliver the baby if I had to keep fighting through the pain too much longer.

I was so pissed to finally agree to do this and then the shot itself hurt like hell! My whole attitude changed after the shot and I felt it blocking up at times, sending me into panic and eventually I was throwing up from the medicine in the epidural. I was a mess and both the baby and my own vitals were struggling. I had been in total control before and now I was in the same pain--but in different places and now I couldn't even feel what I needed to feel or control my own body--plus I was sick! After 29 hours and rounding the clock at 9pm, my vitals began to have serious issues. My doctor explained that I no longer had any choice in the matter and I was wheeled down quickly to the O.R. where an emergency C-section was to be performed. Mark was with me and I was so grateful for that. I vividly remember the doctor cutting me open and feeling the burning sensation. When I screamed, I was put out in a snap by the anesthesiologist.

    The next thing I knew, I was waking up to see Mark holding the baby--our baby boy- right near my face where I could see and touch him. I was extremely groggy and had to hold onto my one hand with the other hand in order to touch him with any control. He was so precious and perfect, with a bruise on his little head from the long labor and from trying to get into the world. It's an amazing moment to meet your baby for the first time, and one you can perhaps only truly appreciate if you are lucky enough to experience the gift of having children. Even if you are able to just be present in a room where an innocent and pure new life begins, it's incredibly special and unforgettable.

    I eventually awoke in the recovery room, thinking I had only been asleep for fifteen minutes. The nurses told me that it was well after midnight and that when I could move my legs, I would be allowed to get back to the room and to my baby. I was so eager to see the baby and Mark, but to my horror, I was paralyzed. I was terrified but the nurses reassured me that it was only temporary. I felt like the epidural that they had given me was finally working now that I didn't need or want it at all. I wanted to get to my baby, not sit down in some recovery room! I mentally forced my legs to move and insisted that the nurse wheel me to my room so that I could see my baby. When I got to the room, Mark was in the dark, sleeping on the cot next to the bed. I could hear crying down the hall and instinctively knew it was my baby. Sure enough, the crying came closer and seconds later he was in my arms. The nurse said that he would be ready to eat and that I should try nursing. I didn't have a clue how to do this besides what I had seen other women do, and Gini with Karlee, so I gave it a shot. It was easier than I had thought it would be, and he began sucking immediately. I will never forget his eyes, staring up at me in that moment. The bond that takes place during this time is amazing. My boobs were as big as his head and I felt hot, tired and beyond heavy. The nurse left the room and when she did, Mark burst into tears, apologizing and telling me how scared he had been during the whole medical ordeal, and that he thought I wasn't going to make it through delivery. He apologized for the fights and for his part in everything. He was in awe of the whole experience and I knew he was sincere and I was genuinely glad to have him there beside me.

 I would be in the hospital for five more days, and Mark was only able to stay for the first three of them. The Cubs were calling for him to come back and he had to leave me before I could go home, and even before we had settled on a name. We had a list of names like Luke, Hunter, Keenan, Liam, and Laird…but the little guy didn't look like any of those names. On the way to the airport, Mark called me and out of nowhere said, "What about Bryce?" And so it was! Mark headed back to Chicago that day a proud father to our baby boy, Bryce James. But it would be some time before I could call him what I consider a true dad.

 I surprised Mark three weeks later by flying out with Bryce for our first Cubs game at Wrigley Field. Chicago fans welcomed us with gifts from strangers in the stands, and people all over seemed to find ways to show their love and support to Mark and his family. I remember my first Cubs game vividly and I certainly couldn't believe the crowd! Everyone stood up on their feet for nearly every play. These were the wildest, craziest, and most loyal and passionate fans I had ever seen. They seemed to all be drinking beer, totally casual and relaxed, and focused on every pitch and play of the game. At first, this annoyed me a little. I was stuck in my seat with an infant nursing or sleeping on my lap. Mark would be up to bat and I would only know what was going on because of people's reactions, not because I could see him myself. I got used to it, and before long I was standing like the rest of 'em, cheering and singing the Cubs song to celebrate each victory. I came to love Chicago and everything about it. The city, the people and yes, the Cubs!

    Being a mom and traveling on the road with the Chicago Cubs and a baby was quite an adventure. It's still amazing to me the amount of stuff a baby needs to have to go anywhere! Being on planes and ripping through airports for young kids can be an education all its own and truly builds confidence in them. I watched Bryce learn to walk with his miniature, rolling suitcase in the American Airlines terminal. He had his little captain hat on and followed me through the airport and right onto the plane. He would look up when we got on and then count the numbers until we got to his seat. Occasionally, we would fly first class and the times we didn't, he would still try to sit there anyway, and would get mad out loud when I would tell him that we had different seats in the back. It was embarrassing in some regards, but equally hilarious in my mind.

    I have a strong bond with Bryce from it being just the two of us for the majority of the time from the beginning of his life. MLB baseball can be tough on any relationship, and especially so when you have kids in the equation. Mark was with the team or on the road 8 months of the year, and with baseball being such a mental sport, he didn't have much left when it came to Bryce and me, or having the patience for the everyday ups-and-downs of a family. With the instability of my own childhood always in the back of my mind, I felt it was important for us to give our child a stable home with a dog and a daily sense of consistency and stability. I didn't think that traveling and following Mark around the country was a healthy way to raise a child. After all, this was Mark's career, not Bryce's, and he deserved better. We eventually settled into a proper home down in San Diego. Mark and I made the decision to try not to go more than two weeks without seeing each other. Mark had a strict routine for himself, though, and I could tell that when Bryce and I would visit, we would take him out of his routine and this was sometimes good as well as bad.

It was in Mark's first year on the Cubs, and under the manager Dusty Baker, that the Cubs went to the Playoffs. That memorable season they were initially up three games to one in the best of 7 game Playoff series. I was in the stadium for every pitch and play and even the night that the Cubs fan, Steve Bartman caught the infamous foul ball from his seat in the stands that sent outfielder Moises Alou into seeing red and left the rest of the team and fans home with broken hearts. They had been 5 outs away from their first trip to the World Series since 1945. The Cubs never seemed to recover and went on to lose the National League Pennant to the Florida Marlins. There wasn't a sound in the stadium when the last out was made against the Cubs that fall evening. The other team was jumping up and down in the center of the field. There were Cubs fans of all ages just sitting in disbelief and utter devastation. I remember old people crying with their faces in their hands, having lived their whole lives at the mere hope of seeing the Cubs play in the World Series. I was also in shock and certainly sad for Mark, but really sad for all these lifelong fans that were so loyal, passionate and crazy about their team. I wanted Mark and the team to win for them!

As most people know, Chicago has two baseball teams and the rivalry between them is one that reminds me of the intense college rivalry between UCLA and USC. Cross-town rivals. You are a fan of one or the other--never both! I actually got into a fistfight with one of the White Sox fans who got belligerent and pushed me. I'm not proud of it whatsoever! Anyway, we got word that the wives of the White Sox players wanted to challenge the Cubs wives to a softball game on Wrigley Field. Of course I was all over this and a few of the other "wives" were as well. The guys were totally behind us and we began practicing and trying our best to get some of the girls comfortable with just throwing and catching the ball. It was a ton of fun being out on the field with the guys and all the girls together. I'm not sure any of us realized how awesome of a time that was for everyone until I think about it and look back on it even in this moment. Wrigley Field is a special place and the Cubs became close to my heart. So, I was determined not to lose--especially against our ultimate rivals and on that cherished field! When it came to game time, we had done all we could do to prepare the girls. We even had our own jerseys and hats. The players on both teams were in the dugouts watching as we ladies took the field and our positions. I heard Moises Alou yell out to me "Don't let anyone else get it Danielle, you get *all* the balls!" It was hilarious how competitive all the guys were for us!

In addition to our Cubs "husbands" there to cheer us on, there were about 15,000 fans in the stadium since this game was taking place right before a real game. We had umpires and everything. Going into the last inning we were up 6-5 and the White Sox wives were at bat. The batter hit a bomb to left-center and I took off after it. Our catcher wasn't the most experienced player, but she wasn't scared of the ball and she was willing to be tough. By the time I got to the ball, the runner had just rounded second and clearly wasn't planning to stop at third. I crow-hopped and aimed for home plate. I had aimed it to hopefully do a one-hop right into the catcher's glove at about her waist and without too much on it. She took the throw like a champ and we got the last out at home plate--shutting them down 6-5. It was truly awesome winning a game against our cross-town rivals on Wrigley field! Go Cubs!

Mark has since played on other teams and has crossed paths with guys that played for the White Sox that year. He will tell me about the things they say that they always remember…how intense I was and how serious I was taking the "just for fun" game that day between the wives. We have laughed about that a lot. I still laugh at how serious Moises Alou was taking it, yelling at me before every hitter, and insisting that I hustle and get every ball. He is one of my favorite players to this day.

Mark was eventually traded to St. Louis to play for the Cardinals after a couple seasons with the Cubs. He was happy to have the opportunity, of course, but sad to leave the Cubs and such an amazing city. Chicago treated us like rock stars and boy do they love their Cubs! The food and people were second to none and when I ask Mark today what was his favorite team to play for, he has never said anything other than "Cubs!" It was my favorite as well. Once a Cubs fan, always a Cubs fan. St. Louis was very welcoming to us, though, and the stadium--even before they rebuilt it was nice. The kids' facility was really nice and the players and their wives were warm and welcoming.

The memory that stands out most from Mark's time with the Cardinals is the day he "hit for the cycle" by hitting a single, double, triple, and home run in one game. It's not every day and definitely not every player who earns this experience--in fact, fewer than 300 MLB players have ever achieved such a goal. I have only seen it once myself in-person and it was the day with Mark at Busch Stadium. Bryce and I were pulling into the stadium when we heard the crowd go wild. As I was stepping out of the car, a parking attendant said to me, "That commotion is for Mark! He just hit a home run!" I quickly grabbed Bryce and we ran to where we could see Mark just rounding third and heading home It was a really hot day, and not too many family members were in the regular seats. Bryce and I were sitting there, though, when Mark got the last hit that would complete the cycle. It was a triple. When he stopped at third, the crowds were on their feet, cheering, and Mark took his helmet off and tipped it to the roaring crowd. I was standing with Bryce in my arms, beyond proud and telling Bryce to wave at his daddy. Mark looked directly up to us and tipped his helmet again and touched his heart for us. I will never forget how proud and grateful I was to be there in that moment. Of course, Bryce was not even two years old yet, and he didn't really know what Mark had just accomplished, but I knew it was something I would never see again and was so grateful to have Bryce there and part of that experience. The organization gave Mark a solid gold

Rolex with the date of 4-27-05 on the back and the words, *hit for the cycle.* It was amazing.

During these years, Mark's career was center stage and my role was that of full-time mom to Bryce. I loved and relished that role, and Bryce and I are forever bonded through our time together--just the two of us at home and on the road. I admit, though, that I struggled quite a bit with the loss of identity and I grappled to understand what would happen to me and my own career and future. Mark and I were engaged, but not married. I was suddenly a full-time, "single mom" in most ways, who was no longer earning an income and I was quickly becoming less relevant in the fickle and forgetful entertainment and modeling industries. I had worked my way up in my world and was in a position of sacrificing it all for the people I loved in front of me. As a result, I was starting to lose that sense of independence and autonomy that had always fueled me. I couldn't quite figure out how to be a mom in San Diego, traveling constantly to faraway cities to keep Bryce and Mark connected, while still finding a way to pursue the work for myself in L.A. that could ensure my stable future.

My frustrations and confusion about my role in life started to seep into my relationship with Mark. I loved being a mom, but I was fearful that in putting everything aside to be that, I was losing everything else that I had worked so hard for. I kept thinking back to Mark's promise that when our baby was born, he would take over the primary caregiver role in the off-season so that I could keep my own career alive. We were supposed to be a team and support each other's careers. When that didn't happen, I felt embarrassed to be in a position where I was essentially living off someone else. I had fought my whole life to avoid that role, and I know it is what prompted much of my fight against Mark during those times. No matter how much time went by, my dad's voice would come back in my head, and I could almost hear him calling me the Taker I had spent a lifetime refusing to be. Things were different, though, now with a young child depending on me. I could no longer just run off and follow my own passion in order to silence the voice in my head and prove it wrong. And, so, I sat with it and listened to it and felt taunted daily by the idea that I was living in a beautiful home and driving a fancy car that all really belonged to someone else. It made me feel dependent, vulnerable, and confused about my own value and worth. Even worse, I now had the silent voice of my dad paired with the very real and salient voices of Mark's family--convinced I was in Mark's life to take his time, money and even attention away from them.

Mark and I both had strong connections with our own siblings, and couldn't imagine raising Bryce as an only child. We both knew that, no matter what else, we wanted Bryce to have a brother or sister to share his life with. And so, in spite of some concerns with where we were as a couple, we were proactive in deciding to bring our second little shared blessing into the world. After a complicated pregnancy and a difficult C-section delivery, baby Brody Adams completed our family in 2007--four years after it started with his big brother, Bryce. Brody was a huge baby who always reminded me of a puppy with oversized paws. From the day he was born, I could see that Brody would share a special bond with Mark. Mark was the first to hold him, the first to feed him, and just a nurturing presence for Brody from the start. Mark's career was starting to wind down, and he was down to the last few years of an MLB career. He still had to travel, but I could see that he was starting to transfer some of his intensity for his work to a newfound intensity for his boys. This time around, he understood what he had really missed out on with Bryce and he seemed committed to making the most of this second chance to be a real dad from the start. Brody and Mark formed a connection early on. As soon as he could talk, Brody would ask where daddy was when Mark was away. In contrast, it never occurred to Bryce to ask something like that; daddy was usually gone playing baseball, and when he was home it was more of a pleasant but unexpected surprise.

Up until the time Brody was born, the Mark I knew had only lived the classic life of a professional athlete-- away on the road, surrounded by friends and fans, and a constant schedule and regimen. We never really had a chance to live together and have a traditional relationship of any kind. We were always traveling and living life on the road, while dating and even after. We fell in love despite our insane schedules and it always seemed naturally simple until we experienced the conflicts over being thrust into a new world with my pregnancy. After Bryce was born, there wasn't a lot of drama or arguing; we just tried to support and love each other as best we would with the constant divide between us. I had traveled to Mark's games often with Bryce, but when Brody joined the family we traveled much less often. Brody never really experienced life on the road as a baby like Bryce had. The constant physical distance and divide inevitably led to an equally real emotional distance and divide between Mark and me. During our rough times apart and his refusal to communicate about these obvious issues, I would prepare myself mentally to raise the boys alone.

Neither Mark nor I are angels, but I believe in my heart that we are both good people who never meant to hurt one another. Nonetheless, navigating through each other's issues from the past seemed to be our most difficult obstacle. A lot of subtle issues in a relationship only intensify when so many additional pressures come into play. Mark's reluctancy to sit down and communicate on some important issues made things worse. I don't believe any issues Mark and I had would have been insurmountable, but another enormous source of stress for me was that Mark's family never accepted me. In their mind, the "L.A. Gold-digger" had gotten her claws in Mark by getting pregnant with Bryce, and they did all they could to let me know how they felt about that. His family is one of the main reasons I never would set a date for our wedding. I just was not willing to enter into such a toxic family that treated me so poorly; however, I was sure that given time they would see that I loved Mark and wanted nothing else but his love and support in return. It would have been nice to have a real family to share with our boys, but it finally became clear that this was not going to happen. When Mark didn't stick up for me at first, I did my best to be tolerant of his family, however distant. When they started to treat Bryce poorly--moving away from us and ignoring him at Mark's games--I was livid and began giving them something to dislike! It took Mark a long time to see their true colors and to finally have my back the way that he should have all along. I regret that Mark's family never accepted the boys and me. To this day, Mark's parents have never even met Brody. "Their loss" is all I can say to that!

After a year with the Cardinals, Mark went on to play for a few years with the Kansas City Royals, the Minnesota Twins, and Cleveland Indians before retiring altogether in 2010. During Mark's career, he earned the Golden Glove award, which is a true honor when the managers and coaches collectively vote to recognize the single best player in the league at each fielding position. In my mind, he deserved the Golden Glove more than the one time he got it! In addition to his great fielding skills, Mark is also part of an elite group of only a few hundred MLB players who have surpassed 2000+ hits in their careers. He has represented the National League as a shortstop in an All-Star

Game as well. I am proud of Mark for his devotion, dedication, and discipline as a player. He has always been a true class act on the field and in the locker room. I loved being at his side, helping him to get ready for each season. We would start throwing about 7 weeks out from spring training and warmed up into fielding and then hitting. I would often throw batting practice to Mark and other MLB players who lived near us. He always included me and this was something that allowed our friendship to always stay strong.

When Mark retired from baseball, Bryce and Brody were about 6 and 2 years old and there were many adjustments that we had to work through in our relationship. Suddenly, we were thrust into living together for the first time--just the two of us in a grown-up house with a couple of kids and dogs…the whole package. We desperately tried to create a traditional family environment, and there just seemed to be so many obstacles for us to overcome. As I said before, baseball and being on the road is hard on any relationship and was especially hard on ours. There were things that happened that were very difficult for me to let go of and just forget about. Things I could never understand. Besides that, Mark was adjusting to a dramatically different role of stay-at-home dad with me there and two young sons to raise. Mark had never before this had any sense of what it meant to be a real parent--helping with homework, bedtime routines, and just taking care of their daily needs and nurturing. I also was used to being on my own, making decisions independently for the boys and myself, and suddenly there was someone else around who wanted to voice a different opinion.

 I had always hoped that Mark would come around and genuinely attach to the boys even half as much as I had. When he finally did, my heart truly felt complete. After he settled in and adjusted to retirement and to living at home with the boys, he finally came to appreciate what it took to raise them and shape them into the little men they will be someday. I always say: "Anyone can be a father but it takes a man to be a DAD!" Mark's job was difficult and having to leave like he did all the time made it hard for him to ever truly connect with them. He has the ability to disconnect and take on an out-of-sight-out-of-mind mentality when he's on that field or gone somewhere. This is a good and bad quality for a family on both ends. I am just happy that he loves them like he does and that they also love him even more back.

I prayed for us for a long time until it became clear it wasn't in the stars for us to work out the way I thought it could. Mark never seemed to have the same affection for me as he did before I had become pregnant initially. It was hard feeling that distance come between us when it first did and the water under the bridge just became more and more as time went on. When the same issues of doubting his love and loyalty came to bear on our relationship, I finally accepted that I would most likely not be able to give my heart fully to him as my husband. We never did get married and by the time Brody was in kindergarten, we had started living apart. It was an unsaid conversation that we were both committed to raising our boys together and being the best partner and support for each other in that process no matter what. When we finally decided to separate and call off our eternal engagement, we handled every issue and decision privately between the two of us and without needing intervention from attorneys or judges. We have respectfully managed each other's wishes and to this day we work out the boy's schedules flexibly and always with their best interests at heart. I am proud to say that we have never wavered in being focused on being good parents to those boys first and foremost. Mark and I happily sit together at school events, coach the boys' sports teams together, we travel on vacations together as a family at times and plain and simply just do what we need to for these boys.

  Life as a single parent is hard on my heart. While Mark is away, back now working in another city with the MLB as a manager, he is back on the same schedule that leaves me doing the parenting all on my own. Managing these two little lives is intimidating and always a challenge I accept. There isn't a greater privilege on this earth than being their mom. I do everything with them and get to see them daily. I feel for Mark because he is surely missing out on so much right now. I send daily pics, texts and videos to him and hope he knows how much we love and support him. It's important for the boys to see what hard work and dedication look like as they look up to him. The four years that he sat in retirement at home with them were tough on him and the boys weren't learning or seeing what they needed to from him. I love Mark dearly and always will. I never would have chosen to end up in San Diego as a single mother without him but that isn't something I ever controlled or knew I needed to. Just because Mark and I don't have a happily ever after card in our own deck as a couple, shouldn't mean that our boys deserve anything less than that themselves. Many people that know us from the kids' schools or sport teams seem to think that Mark and I are married. I actually take pride in that because it tells me that the love we share for our boys unifies us and allows us to be as good a team as any other parents. We have a peaceful relationship for the most part and people are often in awe of the way we co-parent and especially the way we truly get along. We aren't perfect and we do argue sometimes. We do have disagreements and it's usually me who gets mad because I'm so sensitive and will be quickly frustrated by whatever issue it is at the moment. But, I would never want to hurt or upset Mark or cause him any anxiety. It happens sometimes, and when it does it affects me deeply. I am proud of where we are and that we have not let anyone or anything come between us and our commitment to raising our boys together. I am happy that Mark is the man I had my children with. I am grateful for the gentleness and respect he displays with me even today. There won't be a day that goes by that I don't have his back completely--not only because he is the father of my children, but because he is my friend.

    I have never let myself forget the insecurity and instability I felt as a young child--especially the constant fighting between my parents. To this day, I am shocked and saddened at how many people that separate or divorce and then make it a mission to destroy the other person in front of their children. I refuse to let my boys grow up surrounded by unnecessary stress and strife. Mark and I do our best to model love and respect, and when we argue, we play fair and we do not use our kids or their emotions as pawns. Our boys have never known anything different, and I pray that they never will. They are loved, they know they are loved, and in the end that is all that matters.

Chapter Six

"THE HEART OF MATTERS"

"There is no greater name for a leader than mother or father. There is no leadership more important than parenthood."
-*Sheri L. Dew*

Of all the roles I have taken on in life, "Mom" is of course my favorite and most important title. Children are so unique and special and they each require something different of their parents. And so, as my boys have grown up, I have had to learn every day how to grow right alongside them. I am always working to appreciate and understand them as individuals and in that process, I have to challenge myself to be tolerant and accepting, and to appreciate their strengths while understanding, forgiving, and trying to bolster their weaknesses.

Like most mothers, I can say without doubt that Bryce and Brody are the source of my greatest happiness. That also means that they alone also have the greatest potential to bring me the most sadness when they are challenged, compromised, or stressed. As much as I spent my own life learning to fend for myself, I have never known greater humility than becoming a mother and realizing that my own heart was walking around outside my body. I can do my best to keep them close and to protect them, but at the end of the day my job is to instill in them all that I can so that they will grow into honorable young men who respect themselves and others even when I am not around.

    Whenever I was overwhelmed or confused or facing challenges as a new mother, it was Grandpa Sam that I would find myself turning to consistently for advice and as my role model. His strength and grace and his laugh were so compelling. I would ask my grandfather about basic things like how and what to feed Bryce when he was a baby, and I would also turn to him for help with more challenging aspects of parenting and how to instill the right morals and values from an early age. As always, my grandfather was knowledgeable, comforting, and would never fail to reassure me that I was doing just fine as a mother. I relied on him a lot, and just knowing that he had faith in me allowed me to also have faith in myself. So, when I lost Grandpa Sam unexpectedly just weeks after Bryce turned two years old, I couldn't fathom how I would ever be able to continue on as a mother without him there with his special love and that grin that he had always reserved for only me. I also dreaded the idea of Bryce growing up and never knowing or remembering his Great-Grandpa Sam.

I will never forget the day my grandfather died. I had just spoken with him the day before, and he asked me to please hang a sweatshirt that Judi had left at my house outside on the gate so he could drive down to get it. I kept telling him that I would bring it up for him soon and we would have lunch together instead. But, I was leaving town with Bryce to go visit Mark on the road, so it was not going to happen soon enough. I had just hung Judi's sweatshirt on the gate that morning and pulled out of my driveway when my phone rang with my Grandpa Sam's phone number displayed on the screen. I answered, "Hi Grandpa!" just like every other time that he called, and I went straight into telling him how funny it was that he was calling at that moment. There was a short silence and it was Judi's voice on the phone that said, "Baby, your grandpa passed away last night. I'm not sure how yet or why, but he's gone, baby…" I could feel my body temperature change immediately and I felt weak, nervous, and incredibly anxious all at once. I said that I was on my way.

I sat there in my car simply dumbfounded and started to cry out loud, saying, "grandpa, grandpa, grandpa,..." over and over again. I finally tried to start driving toward his home, but I was crying so hard that I had a hard time seeing the road. I tried calling Mark but there was no answer. I called Jeff, (my camera man that I had always trusted and worked with for years) at his work and when he reached the phone to hear my desperate voice, I could barely explain to him what had happened. He was trying to talk to me calmly and he kept telling me how much my grandpa loved me and that I would be okay. I remember saying that I wasn't okay and wasn't ever going to be okay again without him. I was also worried about Judi. My grandpa had so recently been telling me all the things he had planned for Judi and him and now much he loved her--and me, as well. Jeff was reassuring as always and tried to make sense of it all for me and kept me as calm as possible until I arrived at Grandpa Sam's house.

It was about a thirty-minute drive that felt like hours--and yet, I don't even remember the actual act of driving or steering to make the turns that would get me there. I was dizzy and lost when I arrived. I walked straight through the door and fell to the floor in the entry. But in the face of such despair, I instinctually just switched into that familiar mode of tend and befriend as soon as I saw Judi enter the room. I immediately started telling Judi how much Grandpa Sam loved her and all the things he had just shared with me the day before. He was so selfless and was only concerned about her and her happiness-and I knew that making her happy was what truly made him happy. She came down the stairs and held me and I held her right back. She was crying quietly and I was sobbing and trying to understand it all. But trying to be strong for Judi helped me to be strong for both of us and I tried to collect myself so that I could help her with arrangements and decisions.

    I didn't realize that my grandpa's body was still in the house until Judi's sister asked me to go upstairs with her to say goodbye to him. I was in shock at first, but she convinced me that I would feel better if I went upstairs. I agreed and followed her to his room. I had never seen someone I loved like that, and it was surreal for me to see him lying in bed looking so peaceful. I remember his left hand was clutched in a fist over his heart--in my mind, as if he didn't want anyone taking his wedding ring off his finger. I sat at his side with mixed feelings. I was mad at God for taking him because I knew he still had things he wanted to do, plans he made, and that he was absolutely supposed to walk me down the aisle someday! I missed him desperately already and told him I needed him, told him I loved him and asked him not to leave me ever. I kissed him and finally made myself leave the room. I sat on the stairs, sobbing into my lap while Judi made calls and waited for someone to come and take his body. It was one of the very worst days of my life.

I spoke to over 150 people at my Grandpa Sam's funeral and read a letter that he had written to Bryce when he was 1 ½ years old. Someday, Bryce will realize that this letter is one of the greatest and most important gifts he will ever receive in life from anyone. One of my greatest regrets is that the boys didn't get to truly know their Great-Grandpa Sam. He died when Bryce had just turned two and way before Brody was even thought of. I will share his wisdom, my memories, and his letter periodically with Bryce and Brody as they grow. I pray his words can penetrate into their hearts as they always have mine.

I couldn't fathom moving forward without my grandfather. But, as anyone who has suffered loss of a loved one knows, I had no choice but to keep moving forward. At a time when I felt empty and alone, it was the need to care for Bryce and make sure that he himself never felt empty or alone that kept me focused on my purpose and reason for being alive. I still relied heavily on Grandpa Sam and talked to him constantly and I continued to feel his presence in my life then and ever since. He has been my model of a stable, moral, safe, and loving adult, and I was blessed to have had him in my life. I did my best to move forward--with the memory of Grandpa Sam and the need to tend to Bryce as my driving forces.

Even though the boys had lost their great-grandfather, they were also blessed now with a wonderful grandmother. Over time, my mom had started to come back into my life and we forged a tentative relationship that was focused primarily on our shared love for Bryce and Brody. I came to recognize that my mom has a huge heart and never intentionally chose to hurt me or anyone else. I knew her guilt had shackled her soul throughout the years when it came to Sadie and I and our somewhat motherless childhood. But I love her and I forgave her for the past and I hope that she has forgiven herself as well. She evolved into a tremendous grandmother and my boys have always been crazy about their "Grandma Debbie." To watch her with my kids can always make me smile; she has never seemed happier than when she's playing and engaged with them. God bless my mom for fighting to take control of her life, and in doing so, giving my boys the greatest gift of all: the simple, pure, and true love that only a real grandma can offer. I felt they needed this family connection more than ever given that Mark's family was not engaged in their lives whatsoever.

Although Bryce had grown up as my little sidekick on the road with the MLB and even on some of my own film or modeling projects for the first couple years of his life, Brody's birth when Bryce was 4 years old really signaled a new chapter in my life. His arrival marked a shift away from many of my personal and professional goals and I began to focus on establishing a more conventional and stable home and life for the boys. Bryce had always been easy-going and flexible, but then Brody came along and gave me the proverbial run for my money! It's amazing to me how incredibly different two little beings can look and act even though they come from the same parents.

Brody is tough as nails, though sensitive as well, but he will only show that softer side in his own time and to a select few people. He had a rough pregnancy, a rough delivery, and he fought to be here and now seems to keep fighting sometimes even when nobody is against him. He is still young, but nobody can break Brody down--even when he needs to be put in his place unfortunately. If I send him to his room for being difficult or disrespectful, and make the mistake of telling him to "stay there until you can say you are sorry," he might very well stay in his room until the next morning if I let him! While he can be stubborn and strong with us at home, he also has an enormous heart and can be incredibly sweet, kind, and very well-mannered. I love him for the duality I see in him. I know we share this tendency toward extremes and that we will have our share of intense struggles and intense successes together because of it. My mom jokes that Brody is exactly like me at the same age, so I am just relieved that he is already in elementary school and he hasn't even once crashed my car into a tree to prove a point!

    I love being his mom and I love it when he wants to cuddle; Brody doesn't give out kisses or hugs all that often, so when he does, I am all about it. Brody has an easy and natural confidence and a maturity beyond his years. He loves his dad more than anyone, and the two of them could be twins--with Brody simply smaller and wearing glasses. Brody is a natural athlete and is incredible on a skateboard and fearless in the water where he was already catching waves on a surfboard alone by kindergarten. He has a killer instinct and focus combined with a natural athletic talent, and his potential seems endless. Brody is bold and independent and fearless and I love him for all of it.

As Bryce and Brody started to grow up and attend elementary school, I continued to evolve alongside them in my own role as mother. As I step back and look at our life, I know that I haven't always been the traditional mother in some respects, and plenty of times have felt that other mothers would want to make me feel inferior because of that. I take pride in knowing that I always put the best interest of my boys first and we prioritize what matters most to us as a family in everything we do in life. It's true that my boys show up at school sometimes having surfed at 5 am and skateboarded with the dogs down to the village for breakfast before they are dropped off at school with wet hair. Their homework is done, they had a good night sleep, they know they are loved and they have great energy to start their day that is fueled by ocean, fresh air, and exercise. Life is short and precious and I feel good about how we allocate our time and energies.

To be fair...have I ever forgotten to send in a piece of fruit that corresponds with the letter of the week for the class fruit salad? Absolutely. Needed a reminder…or two…or three…to get the permission slip turned in for a field trip? Perhaps. Managed for Bryce to make it to middle school without adding Room Mom to my own resume? Indeed. Driven the kids to school only to find classes are canceled for parent conferences? Not that I will admit! But, my kids' learning, emotional stability, and all-around health and wellness are of absolute critical importance for me and I focus always and intently on those issues. It's true that sometimes the smaller organizational details get overlooked and I have found it discouraging at times when a parent seems to relish finding a way to try to shame me for that. Much worse, though, are the mothers who seem intent on humiliating a child in front of his classmates--instead of subtly asking him if he remembered his green apple to celebrate Johnny Appleseed's birthday or finding a way to be gracious and kind.

 Luckily, my boys seem to have adopted my same indifference to some of these school routines and they don't seem to be impacted if they have to improvise now and then. However, it does infuriate me as a mother to know that some adults are so petty as to want to make a child feel small for no good reason. It has happened more times that it should at school over the years, and I find it shameful when grown parents seem to enjoy putting children in such a position. Bullies exist at every age and position in life and I have never been able to tolerate bullies. This is absolutely one of the greatest challenges as a mother…I want to fight and protect my children from every insult or injury, but I also want to model respect and control for them and not let unkind people control my emotions or choices. So, my best strategy is to jokingly dismiss these mean-spirited mothers as "Momsters" in my head and try to remind myself that I can only control myself and my own effort and attitude.

    I know that I get up each and every day and do my very best for these boys. And my boys are okay with that and I am okay with that. I believe we all have our strengths and interests and that we should tap into these to maximize the effectiveness of what we do with our time. I believe I am best suited to mentor and coach the kids on the fields or courts and in other athletic settings and I allocate my time accordingly. I am supposedly the first woman to serve as the manager and head coach of a Majors Little League team in our city and also as an assistant coach of the league All-Star team. I am not sure if that is true, but I agree to coach whenever I can work it into my schedule, because I cherish my time with the kids in these settings where I know I add value. I never sit in judgment of the many moms that have never coached a team in their life. I am grateful to the parents who trust me and appreciate me for what I do for kids on the fields and courts--just like I appreciate the parents who do the same for my kids when they help in the classrooms and serve on committees at school.

Beyond the trivial challenges of parenthood, every mother knows that our role can actually be downright scary and overwhelming at times. It's even scarier for me when I make myself accept the fact that there are so many things that I can't control in my own life--let alone in my children's lives. We live in a rough world right now, with terrorism and school shootings and random violence seeming to dominate the headlines. I wonder and worry for them beyond just keeping them physically healthy and protected in their daily routines. I believe that the little things we do our best to teach them mean so much more: Kindness, patience, love, forgiveness, honesty, as well as knowing how to protect themselves. They are quite literally our future. Without lessons and examples being intentionally demonstrated for them, where will their values and morals come from? An app? Not in my house. I constantly remind Bryce and Brody that the only thing in life that we truly control is our own attitude and efforts. I feel that is a life lesson that really resonates with me and I truly hope they will always remember those words when they feel up against obstacles or challenges in their own lives.

Bryce had to learn this life lesson too early when he was only six years old. What started out as a regular day in 2009 quickly turned terrifying for our family. I had just gotten out of the water after surfing one morning, when Mark called and said that Bryce was suddenly very sick and was crying for me. I hurried home to find Bryce on the bathroom floor, vomiting and with a gray coloration to his skin. He was moaning and said that he had pains in his chest. I could tell something was extremely wrong, but I had no idea as to the source of the problem. He had been healthy and normal when I left the house a couple hours earlier that morning. I had never seen him throw up like that and even his vomit looked really unusual. His skin was pale and getting more gray and clammy with each passing minute. I scooped him up quickly and took him directly to my truck. I drove him fast to the hospital and talked sternly to Bryce the whole way, trying to keep him conscious and aware and connected to me. When I pulled up to the entrance of the emergency room, I ran him in and as usual, they wanted me to fill out all sorts of paperwork. The gentlemen checking us in noticed that Bryce's skin had gone through three shades of color since we walked through the door and he rushed us back immediately. A nurse met us on the other side of the door and quickly began taking his weight and getting information from me. I was focused on Bryce and keeping him calm and as comfortable as I could. I had him on my lap, my hands wrapped around him and folded tight on his chest. I could feel his heart beating fast and even made mention to the nurse about it. The nurse quickly moved on to the next step of taking his heart rate and blood pressure. It was at this time that she left the room without saying a word, and I told Bryce that she was probably going to come back and take his blood and that he would need to be brave because it might hurt a little. I try to be straightforward with my boys about things like that, so they always believe I will be respectful and honest with them--even when it hurts. I thought the nurse had left the room to go get what was needed in order to draw a blood sample. I just talked and tried to distract Bryce in hopes of keeping him calm. I had not even noticed the monitor above Bryce and that it reflected how unstable he truly was. I only knew that he was completely lethargic at this point, very pale, and his eyes seemed glazed over. My son was fading away right in front of my eyes. He went from talking to almost imperceptibly nodding and then simply to nothing.

The gravity and severity of the situation was just sinking in when a whole medical team came crushing into our room, calling out, "Give us a little room mom, please step aside!" A bucket of ice came flying over my shoulder onto Bryce and I slid back off the bed and was pushed to the outskirts of the room. It was then that I noticed the crash cart being pushed into the room. I looked up to the monitor and saw that his little heart was beating at 248 beats per minute. I nearly fainted when very soon after that the beeps and monitor flat-lined. I looked away from the monitor and back to Bryce. His bright bluish and green eyes were gray, his skin was white with a gray hue and he was completely still. His little body was lifeless except for the unnatural movements that came from the doctors as they worked to resuscitate him. They were calling out things I couldn't comprehend and then gave him a shot right into his chest. I fell to my knees on the floor and a nurse came to me and said, "Sweetie, you are going to pass out. Your son has a heart problem and they will do all they can. You are going to pass out." I remember vividly that feeling of nearly passing out and I refused and fought it with everything I had. I felt like there was a pole behind me that I slid down and I was using it to hold my balance. I crawled to the bathroom--which was straight across from the curtained room that Bryce was in. I remember thinking, "You can't pass out! Bryce needs you, you can't leave him and you can't let him leave you!" I made it to the bathroom on my hands and knees. I crawled to the sink and pulled myself up and turned the water on. I saw myself in the mirror and couldn't believe this was happening for real. I splashed water onto my face and neck and then went back down on to my hands and knees. When I tried to stand, I nearly fainted again. I gave in and just stayed on the floor momentarily and started to pray and ask for help, for Bryce's life to be saved, and to please take me instead. "God, please take me not my son, please. I will never ask for anything else from you as long as I live. I will be the best person I can be always and do my part to leave this world better than when I came. Anything else, please don't take my son." I said this out loud and over and over again. I was folded over my knees, my forehead now pressed on the floor of the bathroom. I had to get back to Bryce but I felt paralyzed. I turned to the door and crawled out of the bathroom and over to his curtained area. I could see the wheels of the crash cart behind the curtain and could see them working on Bryce. I reached up and held his foot and called out to him out loud, "Brycey, mommy is here…, don't you leave me baby! Come back here to mommy Brycey!" I felt his foot move and the monitor began to pick up his heartbeat once again.

    I quickly called my sister Sadie who now had her M.D. and was doing some medical rotations in San Diego. I asked her to come immediately to the hospital. She asked me a few questions and which meds they had given Bryce. She couldn't believe it and was on her way while we were talking. I was shaking and asked her to hurry. I went and sat beside Bryce at this time, and now only a nurse and one doctor were still in the room. The doctor told me that Bryce had a heart condition which would require surgery. He told me that he had an extra passage of electricity in his heart and that there were different conditions that the extra passage could be causing. He made the decision to transfer Bryce to the children's specialty hospital as soon as he stabilized enough to be transported. I finally called Mark at this time and told him what had taken place, I asked him to please get a babysitter for Brody and to come to the hospital. He was shocked and we were both crying and he said he would be there immediately.

I sat next to Bryce who was finally now conscious and alert. I picked up his little pale hand in mine and watched as the color returned to fill back into his eyes. He was exhausted but he struggled to say to me, "Mommy, where did you go?" I said, "What do you mean, buddy? I was right here all along, right here at your side. Mommy would never leave you and I was right here." He said, "No you weren't Mommy, I was yelling for you and looking everywhere for you and you weren't there." I said, "Where is there baby?" He said that he had been running across grass and he was alone there, searching and scared because he couldn't find me anywhere. It was beyond awful to hear this and it was in that moment that I realized why some parents who lose children don't want to live themselves. It wouldn't be because of the depression of going on living without them, as much as it would be the need to be wherever your child had gone and to not allow them to be alone. I thought to myself in that moment that I would never allow him to go alone and that if this were something that could take him for good, that I would go with him. I hurt and could only cry when he said how scared he was alone and looking for me. Tears ran down my helpless face as I reassured him that I was right there and that he would always have me. He told me that he could hear me calling for him and he turned and ran in the direction that he could hear me. He voiced to me that he thought he was dying. I told him that he was right there and that whatever he would have to do or go through, that I would be right there at his side to help him through it.

  When Sadie showed up, I was relieved and glad that someone could deal with the doctors besides me. None of them could give me straight answers on what was going on or if this was going to happen ever again. I was worried that Bryce was a little ticking time bomb and that I couldn't look away or let go of him for fear that he could go off at any moment. My sister explained that the emergency room doctors are primarily there to stabilize the situation and I was beyond grateful that they did exactly that. Sadie got as much information as she could and then began trying to explain and translate for me. I remember telling her that if Bryce needed a heart that she would need to make sure that they would take mine. I was serious and actually happy to do this. I told her that they would need to take my heart, and I know she understood. Bryce and I share a rare blood type and can only take blood from people with the same type as us. I just assumed that if he needed a heart or if the situation could possibly mean life or death for him, that he would unquestionably be taking my heart. I know it may sound crazy and outlandish, but it was the simplest, most relieving decision I have ever made. I actually even felt happy at the thought of it and as if I had lived my whole life to do just that for my son. It would have been my life purpose and the most rewarding one I could think of. Any parent will agree with me that when you have children, you will give your life for them without a second thought. Simple, and in this situation, I actually thought that maybe I could do exactly that. I had already asked God to save Bryce and he was saved. I asked him to take me instead, and I was fully prepared for the possibility that this would in fact be my destiny.

  We were transferred later that day over to Children's Hospital, where we met with a cardiologist who recommended that Bryce be scheduled for heart surgery. There are always the obvious risks of any surgery, but the dangers of the non-surgical route seemed much worse, so we scheduled a date and proceeded from there. In the meantime, Bryce acted fine and seemed quite normal and like himself. I asked many questions and did my research and came to understand that Bryce had a condition called Wolff-Parkinson-White syndrome. It is characterized by abnormal electrical pathways in the heart that cause a disruption of the heart's normal rhythm. People born with this have an extra connection in the heart, called an accessory pathway, that allows electrical signals to bypass the atrioventricular node and move from the atria to the ventricles faster than usual. This extra connection can disrupt the coordinated movement of electrical signals through the heart, leading to an abnormally fast heartbeat. Symptoms of this are very similar to a heart attack and can lead to cardiac arrest and sudden death. Thank God that Bryce's circumstances were as they were, and his heart showed this dysfunction when he was young enough to recover from it.

We have all seen a news story about a seemingly healthy high school athlete running down a court of field and then just falling down dead. WPWS is often one of the underlying heart conditions responsible for such horrifying stories. Unfortunately, it's not a condition that is usually detected until the individual has an actual attack or episode like Bryce did. As awful as the situation was, I am so grateful for the fact that the crisis allowed is to discover Bryce's heart condition early in life and that we would now have a chance to fix it. I have since come to learn that Sudden Cardiac Arrest (SCA) is the number one killer of high school student athletes. In some respects the crisis that our family endured was a gift and a warning sign that I know, tragically, some families will never get. Various nonprofit organizations, however, are now devoted to providing free screenings for all young athletes. There is also legislation pending here in California for more advocacy and proactive measures for education and identification of heart anomalies. I hope that anyone who loves a young person will keep this in mind and take advantage of screenings that might be available in your area.

Looking back now, I do feel lucky that Bryce had his first episode at such an early age and was able to receive quick and effective medical intervention and that we could plan and prepare for the major surgery. However, there are no words to describe the feelings I had when the day of Bryce's heart surgery finally arrived. It was scheduled for one week out after the initial onset and attack. After a long morning of surgical preparations, I was sitting on the hospital bed with him when they came to the pre-op room to take him away. The nurse agreed that I could stay on the bed and ride along with him until we reached the operating room. Mark walked alongside us and Bryce was holding onto me so tightly. He had been calm up to that point, but he began to panic a little as we rolled further and further down the hall. I was whispering in his ear and telling him that I was right there, asking him to just breathe with me. "I'm right here baby, I'm not going anywhere, you'll be okay, my angel." Bryce was saying my name over and over, "Mommy, mommy, mommy, mommy, don't leave me, mommy, don't leave me" as fast as he could through his tears. I told him that if he needed to cry, he could. He was trying to be so brave for us. I didn't want to let go at all or ever, and knowing that I had to do so upset me immensely. I was feeling so helpless and wanted so badly to take any and all of it for him instead. The anesthesiologist saw his panic and put something into his IV to help calm him. In a few seconds, Bryce was drowsy but still crying. I was getting frustrated that he was still awake and having so much emotional discomfort. I walked him all the way into the operating room. They laid him on the surgical table, drowsy but still totally conscious. The anesthesiologist said to kiss Bryce one more time and that he would be asleep. I kissed him on the lips and forehead and he was quiet and peaceful in seconds.

It was so hard to leave my little boy in the eerily high-tech and cold operating room, not knowing what could happen. I wanted to be the one laying there, not Bryce. The surgery would take up to 5 hours and Mark, Sadie, and I waited nervously down the hall in the waiting room for what felt like a lifetime.

9-30-09

"I was asking you to breathe with me and letting you know how much I love you. I was trying so hard not to show you that I was crying, this was the hardest! My heart broke when you were this scared. After the anesthesiologist gave you more sedation, you were calm, tears were still falling down your cheeks from your scared eyes, but calm. They took you from the gurney to the operating table, you were calm, looking all around and still responsive. You were in good hands, I felt this and the energy was positive and confident. I was so proud and didn't want to leave you. They gave your Dad and I a moment to kiss you before they put you all the way under. I kissed you and away you went, into

the clouds. I am so proud of you and so happy to have this behind us. You and your brother are the most important little souls in my life. I would have given you my heart if you needed one. Your heart is all better now, you will heal from now and be back to normal sooner than later. You are such a blessed little boy, growing healthy and strong both physically as well as mentally. You are a good person, Bryce. I love you and need to tend to you right now. You are waking up from your surgery and are feeling a bit nauseous. I am so proud and humbled."

An experience like this will humble any person, let alone a parent. I learned through this ordeal that there are no words for how helpless a parent feels when the health and safety of your child is out of your control. I also learned how grateful a parent may feel when blessed enough to safely reach the end of dangerous but well-lit tunnel with their child right alongside them. When a child is scared or hurting, there is nowhere for a parent to walk but forward with strength in the face of traumatic circumstances in life. Stepping side-to-side, fighting, denying, or panicking will only make it scarier for the child and unproductive or even counterproductive for the parent. The familiar drive to "tend and befriend" makes a lot of sense to me and seems to better describe my instinctual response in this instance and the response of most mothers at times of extreme stress or crisis.

Tending to Bryce through this ordeal and seeing how much he relied on me for security and stability helped keep us both strong. His trust and faith in me kept me calm and focused. I did the only thing I knew and gave him my heart in every way that I could when his own heart failed him. In return he inspired me by showing me the beauty of true resiliency, the unmeasured strength, the innocence, and the unwavering bravery of what it means to be a child.

I believe that our children sometimes act as our little mirrors. They show us who we really are in all sorts of situations, and also who we have the potential of being--for good and for bad. They force us to test our character daily and when they are in danger, they show us how helpless we truly are--but with that, also the ultimate power of love. I look at my boys, I watch them breathing while they sleep, watch them laughing, watch them when they fight and when they are nestled in my arms. I feed off their energy and innocence. I am humbled and amazed daily at how lucky I am to have them in my life. Everything else in life at this point is extra. They challenge me more than any sport, reward me more than any paycheck, and feed my soul in ways nothing and nobody else ever could. They are the only reason my own health or other circumstances ever even intimidate me. On my worst days, I have fought to live for them. I know if I'm not here they will be okay and flourish nonetheless, but selfishly, I don't ever want to leave them while they're still little and finding their ways. I want to see them grow, be there to wipe their tears or to cheer them on when they cross home plate. They are amazing little creatures and sometimes when I look at them, I wonder what I did so right to deserve them in my life.

Chapter Seven

"IT'S NOT ABOUT THE BELT"

"There is no comfort in the growth zone and no growth in the comfort zone"
-Unknown

When I was growing up, I never had anyone in my life that did martial arts. I was nonetheless always enamored with fighting movies and TV shows like "Kung Fu" with David Carradine and especially "Walker, Texas Ranger" with the legendary Chuck Norris. I don't know when I found the time to watch so many hours of TV, but I was hooked on the fighting genre many years before I even took my first martial arts class. I had practiced Karate in high school and on some level I wanted to be able to protect the people I loved and to do what these guys did in the cool manner that they did it. I was compelled by the good guys, strong and controlled and always coming out on top with the bad guy properly put in his place. At least from my kid perspective, that's how it looked!

I remember watching the very first UFC-1 with Royce Gracie in 1993. I remember his posture and his fierce victory that he seemed to win with ease. I loved how traditional he was, coming out with a gi on, so classy and calm. It didn't matter the size of the guys he fought, he beat them every time. He was a sensation and because of him, Brazilian jiu-jitsu became very popular in this country overnight. Royce is from a family of over 40 members of Gracies who have dedicated their lives to the practice and dissemination of the techniques and philosophy of Gracie jiu-jitsu--making theirs the largest family of athletes in the world.

It was incredibly compelling to me that the founder of the Gracie style of jiu-jitsu, Carlos Gracie, was the smallest and skinniest of the Gracie Brothers--yet he was never defeated, not even by his stronger and younger brothers. He was 135 pounds and had introduced leverage to the already effective art, so that lighter, smaller, and even weaker individuals could defeat heavier, larger, and stronger opponents. The jiu-jitsu system of self-defense teaches this and has proven itself time and time again--as Royce did for the world during the first Ultimate Fighting Championships. I'm not much for starting a fight--and never have been--but I was absolutely captivated by the power of this martial art and its seemingly gentle ways of going about it.

I took my first jiu-jitsu lesson class in Mission Viejo with Chris Brennan, who was a long-time friend and one of the most talented athletes I have ever met. Chris has fought all over and has also competed in the UFC, PRIDE, and King of the Cage contests amongst others. Chris had opened a school up in Mission Viejo called Next Generation. He taught Brazilian jiu-jitsu without the gi and told me that I needed to get on the mats and give it a try. I would drive the hour down from Los Angeles twice a week to train whenever possible. I loved it but was unable to commit due for long due to my many other obligations in Los Angeles.

Years later, my sister Karlee began dating and eventually married Jared, who had been training in jiu-jitsu for years and eventually opened his own school on the island. When I would go over to Kauai to visit my sister, I would tag along with Jared to classes and we would step out and train together in their garage as well. Every time I would return to visit Kauai, the people that I had trained with before had gotten so much better and I would always leave the island feeling frustrated and wanting more. When I got back to California after a trip to Kauai in the summer of 2006, one of the first things on my list was to look around for a reputable local school that taught Brazilian jiu-jitsu. I must have been really putting the vibe out there, because I got a call from a friend one day telling me that I should come take a jiu-jitsu class with him in Encinitas. I told him that I was actually looking for a school, and not long after our conversation, I joined the Gracie Barra Academy.

Brazilian jiu-jitsu is a popular and efficient martial art. It's a combat sport used primarily for self-defense. Most people that think of jiu-jitsu, automatically think of the UFC and cage fighting. Yes, jiu-jitsu is a major player in the MMA world and the most effective martial art should a fight take to the ground. The term jiu-jitsu, however, translates to "the gentle art." It is referred to this way because the art utilizes leverage and technique rather than brute strength. As a woman, this is good news. No matter how tough or strong a woman might be, a man can strike a woman harder than she can strike him. On the ground, though, the playing field becomes a bit more balanced and the techniques and leverages of jiu-jitsu can put even the biggest, toughest guys right to sleep--or send them tapping out!

Jiu-Jitsu for me is a life tool. I would never have imagined a martial art mirroring life with such accuracy as jiu-jitsu does. Just like life, any style of martial art will have many "what-if's" to contemplate for each position or circumstance you might find yourself in. It's in these moments that we learn about ourselves, our strengths, weaknesses, and also what we need to be working on more--both on the inside and the outside. It's a humbling sport and one where you realize as you go, that the more you know, the more you truly don't know. There isn't a time I step on the mats that I don't learn something new--either by way of a new technique, or from my training partner. This martial art is ever evolving and there are so many different ways to mix the techniques and so many ways of attacking.

Jiu-jitsu is challenging, it's tough, it's rewarding, and it personally has offered me a space and many moments and opportunities to better myself as a person. It has offered me the privilege of being part of something bigger than myself, a second family of friends and training peers with whom I could build rapport and share trust and respect. It was intimidating as a newcomer at first, but once I committed to it, it became a source of power that fed my soul, body, and mind. Jiu-jitsu can build the inner strength of a person in ways one can only understand if you train. I personally believe that jiu-jitsu is a special art form, but of course everyone's journey with it will be different.

Being a woman on the mats isn't always as easy as people might think. Most people assume that men take it easy on me--or any woman for that matter. My experience has been that they don't. It is something that takes getting used to, and I have gotten used to it. Everyone who has gone hard on me, I want to thank them because they only made me better. Men don't like getting beaten by women in just about anything. Jiu-jitsu is about leverage and technique beating strength and men learn to truly appreciate and understand that when they roll with a technical female and tap to her.

Some women that I've brought to class to either try it or just to watch can't imagine themselves laying down on their backs and allowing a man to get between their legs so easily. For a jiu-jitsu practitioner, this position is what we refer to as the GUARD. It is a strong position for the person on the bottom and there are countless attacks from the guard. For a woman who hasn't ever trained, watching from the sidelines, the whole thing looks like one big sexual position. They are in shock half the time and later, the value of this position takes on more clarity. To be honest, the positions in jiu-jitsu are relatively uncomfortable. It's a physical chess match in some sense and while training you are always trying to advance positions upon your opponent--hopefully before he or she can see them coming. Your opponent is also doing the same to you, so defense and offense are equally important components of the sport.

    Training day to day and competing offer very different experiences within the sport of jiu-jitsu. You can advance through the belt system the same as anyone else, even if you don't compete at all. In jiu-jitsu, white belt is for beginners, then blue belt, purple belt, brown belt and then finally the black belt. The natural goal when beginning any martial art would be to ultimately obtain the Black Belt. In life, obtaining any goal takes a great dedication, perseverance, commitment, and the ability to start something at the very beginning and see it through to the finish. Too many people are so focused on the position they are striving to obtain rather than taking notice of the moments within that journey. All the steps it takes to get there are just as important as reaching the goal itself. The lessons and some of the best memories are in the moments leading up to your goals. I have heard it said that a Black Belt is just a White Belt who never gave up. I wholeheartedly agree. A black belt to me only signifies the beginning of my education and journey in Brazilian Jiu-Jitsu. I learn something about myself every single time I step on the mat and sometimes it's a white belt I learn it from. I am always humbled by my partners and the time they give me is appreciated.

As I mentioned earlier, everyone's path or journey within this art form is different. There are a few of us that are hooked on the competition aspect of the sport and many who are not. Some people enjoy coming to the class and training only. Competition for me, though, helps what I learn in practice, translate to something more real for me. It offers me a stage to better see myself and exposes my weaknesses so that I may work harder and maximize the potential of whatever I can possibly do or be within this sport. Competition motivates me to raise the bar for myself and forces me to step beyond the comforts of my own school and peers that I feel safe with when I have to compete against strangers. This requires me to step beyond the comforts outside of as well as inside of myself.

When I step on the mats to compete, I let go of a false sense of control and I transition instead to that moment where I take charge. Let's face it, the only thing in life we can control is our attitude. Taking charge and taking control are two very different things. Taking charge allows me to feel alive. The warrior in me comes out and I feel my heart beating in my chest and my body thriving with adrenalin. I am taking charge of that moment and relying on my training to execute and win my fight. I take charge and trust that my hard work and practice will come naturally and pay off. Some people take competition very seriously and for them each fight is a defining moment. For me, defining moments are far and few. Mine are defined by much more substantial moments and circumstances. I love to compete but the outcomes don't make or break me. I always try to compete with class and etiquette. I fight fair-but with every intention to win. I am usually very calm under any kind of pressure and competing in jiu-jitsu is no different.

Women are very technical and usually have to be since many of us train in male dominated schools. We must rely even more so on the technical aspects of jiu-jitsu to advance or dominate our partners. We must flex our brains before our muscles in order to execute on the mats against stronger men who are learning the exact same techniques as us. I actually find that I have more difficulty fighting smaller opponents in competition than I do against larger and heavier opponents. I am always respectfully intimidated by any opponent, but also go into all my matches confident and always fighting for the win. Having been a competitive athlete in other sports, I have learned the formula for what it takes to be a good competitor. I know when to push and when to calm it down during a match. I know how to preserve my energy and to maintain the stamina and strength I need to last a full match.

Most competitive jiu-jitsu matches last between 5-10 minutes. You might naturally think that the 5-minute match might be a better option for a fight. I have fought both and I can say that 5 minutes has proven much more intimidating than 10-minute matches for me personally. There is less time to fix any potential mistakes in a shorter match that feels more like a sprint than a marathon. Many people get pretty winded fighting for 10 minutes straight and I feel that this gives me a chance to prove myself through perseverance. Some things can be very deceiving in jiu-jitsu. I have learned my lessons and usually the hard way. I maintain that I prefer a match with a heavier competitor in a longer 10-minute bout. You wouldn't necessarily hear the same from most jiu-jitsu players, but everyone has their strengths, limitations, and weaknesses.

After years of competing, I have won my fair share of gold medals and lost about four fights total so far. I am a world champion competitor. I have had my finger dislocated as well as my arm popped in an arm bar, losing that fight hurt worse than the other injuries I sustained by far. I am both proud and embarrassed to say that I have thrown up in the sleeve of my gi for fear that the crowd watching would know me as "the girl who threw up!" During an intense match, I knew that I had to vomit, but the closest trash can was straight in front of the stands where spectators were. I turned around and tried keeping it down at first, but was clearly inevitable that it was going to come out. I threw up into the sleeve of my gi and then wiped my hand down my pants. The referee had called a timeout for us to adjust our gi's, in which hers had come undone. When we resumed, I didn't give her the sportsman's handshake that we typically give because I didn't want her to have to touch my hand. From the outside, it looked like I was being un-sportsman-like, but I was only trying to be considerate.

I ended up losing that fight by an advantage. It's an attempt at getting a submission point, not even a full point. It can separate a win from a loss by effort alone. I don't like winning by advantage points and surely didn't like losing by one! I know it sounds a bit cocky to say I don't like winning by an advantage point, because winning is winning. Had it not been for my years spent at UCLA and under the badass coaching of Sue Enquist herself, I might have also thought that a win is a win and I would be happy with it. Sue taught us to win and take the jugular of the opponent and that anything less was a loss. So, naturally, winning for me by an advantage is never good enough. But, losing by an advantage is just awful! Fortunately, at UCLA, we didn't do too much losing. Losing was not accepted, and had there been advantage points in softball, and we ever lost by one, we would have suffered indeed!

I can't stand to lose, but in hindsight, it is in those moments I have learned the most. I have been a competitor all my life and I don't know when the competitive edge will ever leave me. I feel silly sometimes entering jiu-jitsu tournaments, signing up to actually fight another person. The potential of getting seriously injured is always there and still I keep signing up, pushing myself, and testing my abilities and boundaries. There is something about gearing up for a tournament that makes the whole experience of jiu-jitsu different. Getting ready for a tournament and the preparation that goes into it is just as important to me as the tournament itself. The dedication to the training, the mental and physical aspects of it, the commitment it takes to make the proper time for extra training, the fine line of training hard and pushing limits while avoiding injury is critical. It's all part of the process.

    I love the feeling I have getting to the tournament and being able to relax and rely on my preparation. It's like studying hard for a test in school and that feeling of complete calmness you have, almost eager for when the teacher hands you your test. It's the same for me on the mats; I work hard and earn my place to be there. It's probably one reason why I'm always so calm by the time I get there. I know that whatever I have that day has to be good enough. At my level now, every competitor is talented so it's not who wants it more, it's the person who makes the fewest mistakes. I learn more when I lose than when I win. It's just like finding strength through adversity. It hurts to lose… and bad! I spend hours and hours training and preparing off the mats. When I've made a mistake that costs me the tournament, it torments me. I play the critical situation over and over again in my head, getting more pissed by the minute and then I take those emotions back to the mat and do my best to fix it and not let the same mistake happen again in the future. Some of the times when I've been caught in a submission to just be beaten down again and again by the same submission, I start to make that very submission my best attack on someone else. It's an awesome thing about jiu-jitsu, like Master Carlos said, "You either win or learn." It's true. It's the same in life. We win some and lose some and with that, are always learning about others and especially ourselves.

    Jiu-jitsu is a very reflective martial art to everyday life. When we step on the mats and commit to being a practitioner of the art, we are stepping into a lineage of the professors and Masters of that art that have come before us. We are honoring and carrying on their legacy. We are gathering in our lives yet another formidable tool to bear in a time of need--be it physically, mentally or emotionally. Every day on the mats, like in life, is an opportunity to learn. What you absorb from these opportunities and take from them is up to you. What you choose to give back as well is up to you. To believe or think you are in control of things in life or on the mats is a mistake. Taking charge is a better approach than taking control in most situations both on and off the mats. Centering yourself in your own life, finding balance and leveraging certain situations to your benefit is much more conducive to any situation. In jiu-jitsu, people often make the biggest mistake by using all their strength or attempt to control their opponent. If the opponent is smart, they will defend with the least effort possible and wait until the opponent exhausts him or herself before making another move. Eventually, when this happens, the opponent will then apply technique and leverage to advance the position of the person using strength therefore taking charge of the situation in which the other person was intending to control.

Trying to control anything besides your own attitude is a dead end. Chasing people who don't want to be with us or don't love us back is a waste of time and never pays off. Trying to control things in life will only leave you with two things at minimum: yourself and alone. We must give up the idea of control to gain realistic control. We all seek it whether we acknowledge it or not. It's a natural human tendency. Jiu-jitsu has taught me a lot and one of my most valuable lessons of all was to stop trying to control situations or people in my life.

When I first began practicing jiu-jitsu, people would always make comments about how strong I was. I would do my best to outmuscle even the guys in my class to stop them from applying certain techniques like chokes and arm bars to me. I would fight, sometimes "out of control" thinking that I was controlling things enough with my strength for my opponent not to be able to apply their techniques upon me. I looked at it as if I was losing every day, only to realize later that I was being conditioned to leave my strength and need for control off the mats. Learning painfully, as I have always seemed to do, that the more I tried to control someone else, the more mistakes I made and the less control I actually had. This process is a tough one to understand much less give in to. Almost all white belts struggle with this and then gradually while climbing the ranks within jiu-jitsu, it becomes more clear what exactly makes this particular art so effective. For some, this realization comes quickly and for others, the realization is there, but they have a much tougher time giving up the control and trusting in the techniques.

The universe has many different ways of showing us what we are supposed to see or learn at certain times in our lives. We step into the world every day and whether we want it or not, we will learn something. It's our choice how we choose to process what we've learned or how we choose to use it. I have been given many tools in life through different means and lessons learned both through pain and through love. Obstacles are put in front of us that blind us or may knock us right down. I have been blessed to have had these lessons, obstacles and adversity at the times I did. Jiu-jitsu is yet another tool that I now have the privilege of being able to utilize that has helped prepare me for things I had no idea were in my sights. It has humbled me and showed me that the path of least resistance isn't always as it may seem. There is usually a better and more gentle way of going about something that just might be even more effective than what I had originally contemplated or intended on. Practicing this martial art has allowed me to develop more patience for others and more importantly, myself. It's an art where even an inch makes a huge difference. A half inch could mean the blocking of your carotid artery and a submission.

I have been honored to have worked with women conducting anti-rape seminars, with kids in anti-bullying assemblies and classes, and to have instructed kids classes and helped young competitors in their tournaments. Jiu-jitsu has been a vehicle for me to share my message and to help others. It has been a gift I could teach and enjoy and share with my two sons so that they can learn to protect themselves in any precarious situation. It has been a vehicle that has helped me to know myself better and aided my spirit.

Whether your goal is obtaining a black belt or a Masters' degree, or a Ph.D., remember that there is a journey and character qualities that one must possess to obtain each of these things. There are people along the way, whether we acknowledge them or not, that have been sent to us for certain reasons and opportunities. In some instances, adding to our success and aiding or merely inspiring us in our efforts to be something more that we first thought possible. Despite your desired acquisitions, there is much more to this world than your own selfish gain. When I say that, I don't mean financial goals or fame or self-absorption. I am talking about being the best person you can be. To go somewhere and leave it better than when you came, or to inspire someone else to be better than they ever thought they could be. There are a lot of good people out there, great ones even. The world is short of extraordinary people, of true Black Belts. Ph.D.'s in kindness and people with Master's in character. Most of these people fly under the radar, not wearing their black belts for all to see. They are the ones who do their talking with actions. Actions that leave people in awe or with a simple smile. Extraordinary people are the ones who train every day to be extraordinary without even knowing it. They make the conscious effort to do something every day to improve something or someone around them. They train this until it becomes second nature. They practice and demonstrate their character by doing what they say. They are the people who would show up for you in hell with a bucket of ice that wouldn't melt!

I believe that if a person is heathy-minded, then they are capable of anything and certainly at least of being kind. Jiu-jitsu is a gentle sport with stiff consequences. To receive, you need to give. To advance or be anything in it at all you must train. Without a training partner, you are nothing in the art. Jiu-Jitsu isn't a Kata sport. It's a people sport, what we like to call a family. We help one another, share new and different techniques with each other. We give to receive. If more people could do this, with integrity, character, and kindness, this world could surely improve. Jiu-jitsu is full of "what if's." When we are shown one technique, there is always a "What if the guy does this or that?" Life is the same, "What if I had just taken a moment to say this or say that in this way?" and "What if I would have or could have...?" We all could probably say this about hundreds of situations in our lives. Have you ever listened to older people speak of earlier interactions or relationships? Take a moment to actually listen to them, they've been here much longer than us and their accumulated wisdom deserves respect. They have made all the mistakes we possibly haven't yet, and life would sure be easier if we could figure out a way to learn from the wisdom of others instead of learning everything the hard way.

 My hope is that anyone reading this will be compelled and inspired to give any martial art a try. It's not about hitting and kicking or muscling people around to get them to do what you want them to do. It's about strategy, technicality, and leverage. Your greatest strength that will be found deep in your heart when you are fighting for a position on the mats or in life with your partner or anyone for that matter, is defending and refusing to give in or give up to get it. Strength will be needed on those days when all your other tricks aren't working and you feel like giving up but won't! It will probably compel you to show up the very next day and try again and harder. If you can do this, then you will probably leave that next day having peeled yet another layer back to reveal a part of yourself that maybe you didn't even know existed before.

    No matter what it is we are here on earth to learn or do, we are tested and presented with moments, opportunities, and lessons throughout our lives. We don't get to choose where they come from or why, but they come and will surely keep coming. I have had my share of tests, lessons, and even nightmares. I have grown a lot since I began jiu-jitsu and that growth has allowed me to learn to accept certain situations for what they are, rather than fight to try to resist them. I take them in, size them up and step out to address them with my knowledge and other tools at my disposal.

    I give my challenges and tasks all I have got at any given time, maximizing the potential of the opportunity and seeing it as such. I am firm and never willingly give in. I submit when I can, or roll until I've tired out or given my best. This attitude is something I have always possessed, but jiu-jitsu has taught me to polish it and hone it into a craft that I now try to apply to most everything in my life. Whether I'm on the mats training in class with my peers or fighting for a world title, I go hard and straight at it. I face my fears, my wants, and even my loves. Loving another can be the scariest thing in the world. I try to face these things with confidence that my training and time on the mats of life will serve me when I need them most. I didn't always know what compelled me to the particular art of jiu-jitsu or what inside of me motivated that fire and desire to compete. Sometimes we don't get these answers until they are granted to us or we have evolved our vision to clearly see them. I have seen jiu-jitsu transform people's lives and even aid in saving my own.

Chapter Eight

"TWIST OF LYME"

Anyone who has ever seen an episode of *"Monsters Inside Me"* on Animal Planet can maybe imagine my feelings as I sat in the examination room of a specialist's office in the spring of 2010, being questioned about things like: "Have you had a respiratory infection in the past five months? Have you been fatigued? How about any depression? Have you traveled in the past year or two? What is your diet like? Do you have brain fog? Are your joints stiff or painful? Do you have digestive issues or suffer stomach pain? Does your spine have pain? Heart pain? Do you have stress?" It was scary to think in that moment that I could answer yes to all of those questions. I had no idea why I was in such bad shape and I wouldn't find the answer until months later. Looking back and knowing what I know now, I still find it hard to believe that the reason I was sitting there in such dire health could be traced back to the bite of a minuscule tic bug.

It happened in the springtime, when my whole family went out to New York to celebrate Sadie's graduation from medical school. The weather was humid, with rain most days. We had been cooped up in a hotel and I decided to take Bryce out for some fresh air on a little walk through Central Park. Baby Brody stayed behind with family, and Bryce and I borrowed umbrellas from the hotel and headed down the busy streets toward the park. New York is beautiful in the spring, and the rain doesn't slow that city down a bit. It wasn't easy walking side by side down the busy sidewalks with umbrellas. I guess it's better to have one in your hand when everyone else does, if you don't, you will probably get your eye poked out otherwise.

When we reached the park, it was pouring down rain, but there were still quite a few people jogging through the park, seemingly enjoying themselves in spite of the wet and humid conditions. I don't know Central Park all that well, but we were near a merry-go-round that Bryce wanted to ride, but it was closed due to the weather. I suggested a game of hide-and-go-seek instead. We both simultaneously shouted out "one, two, three, NOT IT!" We tried to break that tie with a game of rock, paper, scissors. We usually played it "best out of three," but when Bryce was losing, it quickly became "best out of five" and so forth. I won straight up, though, and we set the boundaries and Bryce went to count. I ended up hiding behind some bushes up against a boulder. It was very wet and I was in tight quarters with the bushes to the front of me, and my back pressed against the boulder. I was knelt down on the grass and dirt and totally submerged in the bushes. It took Bryce a while to find me, and so I was crouched down there for a while. When Bryce finally found me, I was "it" and he took his turn to hide. We did this for a while and then finally decided to head back once the rain started coming down hard again. We strolled back, umbrellas in hand, and enjoyed the rain along the way. It was actually a sweet day in my memory with Bryce, but I walked away with much more than a memory. I also walked away with a tic bite.

    I have always been exceptionally healthy and full of almost too much excessive energy. I'm an early riser and usually a very productive and active person. I have obviously been an athlete all my life, and so my physical self has truly been a main source of survival--financially and mentally as well as emotionally for me. I have channeled my anger, sadness, fears, love, courage, insecurities and just about anything else I could into my sports. It's one of the biggest parts of my existence. To have that physicality threatened by anything, especially an illness or disease of any kind, is something I never could have imagined. I have taken so many precautions throughout my life to stay in top health. I have never willingly tried any drug, or even a cigarette for that matter. I didn't drink alcohol until I was 21, and to this day I am particular and selective about when I choose to drink. I know my body well and at this point in my life I had rarely even had the flu.

After my four days in New York that May, though, I was stricken with a cough that quickly developed into a pneumonia by June. I had been surfing a lot that month since getting back to California, nearly every day, and training jiu-jitsu about 3-4 times per week. I was also riding my horse every morning and training with him. I was dealing with some emotional stress as well as transitional stuff at home and with Mark. A lot was going on, and a lot for me is normal, but I was definitely channeling that into a lot of physical activity. I knew I wasn't feeling well at all, but it takes quite a bit for me to stop and care for myself at all-- let alone go see a doctor. I called Sadie and asked her to please phone in a Z-pack prescription for me. She told me that I would have to go see the doctor myself, because she wasn't allowed to prescribe medications in another state. I finally called my doctor and described the symptoms and also that I had been coughing for weeks and I couldn't seem to shake it. He said he would prescribe me the Z pack but that I would need to follow up with him in person. I agreed, but when I went to see him that Monday, he was over an hour late for the appointment--and I was too cool to wait, so I left. I finished the Z-pack but still I felt as if I hadn't even taken a single pill. I was coughing worse, and now, was finding it hard to even get out of bed in the morning. Totally not me!

    Without really fully realizing it, I was slowing down every day, little by little. At first I would chalk it up to the fact that I was unable to sleep most nights due to the coughing coupled with my emotional stress. One day, my elbows started to itch and I noticed a mild, pink, bumpy rash on the outside of both of them. The rash was hot to the touch and extremely itchy. I kept thinking it was from stress or maybe even the ocean, but it wasn't unbearable so I ignored it the best I could. I remember trying to soothe it with cream and even some Neosporin but neither one took the edge off the itching. The irritation levels would come and go and eventually I started to see the same bumps on the tops of my knees. I was actually sitting on a plane to visit Karlee in Kauai with Bryce and Brody when I first noticed my knees. The slight rash quickly turned into burning, itchy and welted-up patches. I again ignored the pain and did my best not to scratch at my skin.

While we were on Kauai, I noticed that the sun and salt water irritated the rash so much that I was uncomfortable even going in the water. For me, this is unheard of and I knew I was going to have to figure out what was going on. I was training jiu-jitsu in the evenings with Jared, and even my own sweat and the material of my gi were painful on my skin. I could feel my elbows and hips stiffening up and still I kept denying that anything was really wrong. One morning when I woke up on the island, I remember having trouble getting up and out of the bed. My hips were beyond sore and it was difficult for me to lift my feet and take steps. I was shuffling down the hall, and when I went to walk down the steps, I lost my balance and fell forward, catching myself with help from the railing. I looked down at my hands and saw that the rash had spread to my knuckles, wrists, and was now even on the outside of my hips. I was miserable. Still, I kept trying to ignore it and not allow it to ruin my trip with the kids.

Jared and I had planned to take the kids on a little train that day on the south side of the island while my sister went to work. On the way out for the day, I was in so much pain that I finally broke down and asked Jared if he could take me by urgent care to see if they could give me something for relief. He could see the rash all over me and he could even feel the heat emanating when he put his hand over the top of my wrist and knees. There was only one accessible dermatologist on Kauai and I couldn't see him unless I went through the ER first. It's ridiculous, but apparently there was no way around it. I felt bad to leave Jared with all four kids, but I had no choice. I couldn't take the pain I was in for one more painful day or sleepless night.

When I finally got into an exam room, it was four hours later and I could have sworn that the rash got worse by the hour. I think the humidity might have made it worse, or just the process of the whole experience. The doctor finally walked in and he immediately put gloves on. He stayed far away from me, reading the chart and the paper I had filled out a few hours earlier in the waiting room. I was absolutely miserable at this point and asking him for anything to relieve the itching and burning of the rash. He asked me if I had been on a plane recently and I said that I had. He then pulled his chair up to a computer in the room and typed "Scabies" into the internet search engine. He turned the computer toward me so I could see the screen with him, and he proceeded to tell me I had "bed bugs." I can't quite put into words how that resonated with me to hear that I have "bugs" of any kind--let alone "bed bugs" or "scabies." I couldn't have felt dirtier. I was disgusted, embarrassed, and absolutely mortified! I wanted them off me immediately. The doctor kept his distance and I asked with obvious reason if I was contagious? He proceeded to tell me that it was contagious and that I had probably contracted it on the airplane. Even though I had told him that the rash had been on the elbows for quite some time and only recently had it spread to the rest of the areas, he was convinced that it was bed bugs and that they came from traveling. He told me that I could take a prescription to the pharmacy, purchase the creams and whatever else and I should start to feel some relief by that evening. Something didn't make sense. But even then, I didn't want to be near myself or sitting in my own skin! All I could think about were my kids, my sister, Jared, and their kids. Their youngest was only a baby, and here I was, spreading BUGS around their house and everywhere else I had gone!

When Jared came to pick me up, the kids were all excited to tell me about the boars they saw from the train ride. I tried my best to engage with them and listen to their tales from the day. Jared asked me what the doctor had said and I remember not wanting to say a word. I was still in major pain and just told him to please take me back to the house. Once I got there, I began pulling all the linens, showered the kids, and I started administering cream to them and myself. I took every towel in the house, blankets out of the cars, and everything I had touched outside to shake off or clean best I could. I finally told Jared a lighter version of what the doctor had told me. I was searching my arms, knees, anywhere the rash was to see if I could see these bed bugs that I supposedly had. The doctor had said they were near microscopic, but still, I should have been able to see something! I scrubbed myself until I was nearly bleeding and then the burning I felt from the water hitting my skin was torture. I then moved on to scrubbing the kids, and when Karlee came home, I finally told her. She was calm, but I could tell she was a little worried. I kept apologizing and felt awful for having ever gone there in the first place. I immediately changed my flight and left that evening on the red-eye. The creams and whatever else they had given me only irritated the rash and provided absolutely no relief. I couldn't take another sleepless night or another painful day in the sun.

    I landed that next day in San Diego and was greeted by my friend, John, at the airport. John was my driver for a long time and became one of my dear and trusted friends. I felt reassured just seeing his face and I asked him to take me directly to the dermatologist. He took care of me first and then proceeded to take the kids back to the house where their dad was. I sat in the waiting room without an appointment and said that I would sit there until someone could see me. I wasn't leaving. I was in terrible pain. When I finally got back to the examination room, the doctor looked at my rash and immediately said it wasn't bed bugs or scabies. She said it was an unusual rash--being that it was on the outside of all my joints and nothing on the inside of my limbs or arms where most rashes more typically are. She took biopsies of skin from my elbows and I left there with stitches, an itch prescription, and in even more pain than when I came. I felt comforted a little by the fact that I could call my sister and let her know that there were likely no bugs crawling around her house. But, that was about it as far as it went with comfort gained from that visit.

I quickly drove to the pharmacy for the itch cream and some oral medication to help with the pain. I went home, showered, and applied the cream. Once again, the creams did nothing except irritate the rash and burn worse. I lied there at night, agonizing in pain, eager for the next morning to come so I could go back and get something else to try for relief. By this point, my joints under the rash were sore and getting stiffer by the day. My energy level was diminishing and my depression worsened by the day. Each day was progressively worse. I was falling apart from the inside out. My face was breaking out, my healthy skin color was gone, and so was my positive attitude. I couldn't understand.

About 12 days after the biopsy, I received a call from the dermatologist letting me know that the labs had been run repeatedly but had come back "inconclusive." When I explained that my symptoms were worse, I was referred to another specialist. By this time, my joints were the stiffest they had ever been and my overall pain was ranging about an 8 on a scale from 1-10. The itching had been curbed a bit with some cream they had given me on the third try, but the rash was still visible and burned even with the meds. I could barely bend my elbows, couldn't even open a water bottle, and I shuffled when I walked. I was fatigued to a point that when I would lie down, it was too much to even turn on my side or remove my shoes to sleep comfortably. I would lie there, paralyzed sometimes, unable to relax or sleep. I was exhausted beyond description of the word and couldn't understand how to even describe the pain and hopelessness I felt. I would sit on the couch and have to count to ten before I could make myself get up. I was hard on myself, calling myself names under my breath or in my head nonstop. Telling myself how pathetic and weak I was. I refused to give into this new reality and refused to believe there was anything but a mental breakdown taking place. I hated life, hated myself, and hated everything. I wanted to disappear and leave the world I knew. I wanted to hurt myself and punish myself for the thoughts and attitude I was demonstrating within my own company.

    I was falling into a deep depression without knowing it. Depression is something I had heard of, but never bought into. I didn't have a very high opinion of people who claimed they were "depressed." I used to think it was an excuse or just negativity manifesting. I couldn't understand how people could look in perfect health, have money, nice families, healthy kids, and seemingly good lives, and then sit around and complain about being depressed. These people seriously drove me bonkers. I had no respect for them and truthfully stayed clear of their negative vibe.

Suddenly, though, I had a very real understanding of the powerful force of depression. I would find myself having very serious thoughts of taking my life. I would be driving down the road and start picturing myself steering the car straight into the center divider or even off a cliff. I would see it vividly, the situation playing out in my mind, and I would wonder if I would die quickly or if I would suffer. I would think about taking pills or paddling out in the biggest waves I could so that I might drown. I would play out the scenarios in my head--without remorse of my thoughts and I believed the world and even my kids would be better off without me. When the depressive feelings would let up even a little, I would then hate myself for having such horrible and horrendous thoughts. I would feel guilty for the thoughts and for having ever fathomed doing anything like that to my family, my kids, or my close friends. It got to a point where I hated myself when I was suffering the depression and even when I wasn't. I felt fear, hatred, and self-defeat and self-loathing. I didn't know what was happening and I was alone and embarrassed for the feelings and thoughts I was experiencing. I would call Courtenay and talk to her about this and I remember a few times, her showing up at my house, worried sick that I would actually do something. It was scary, frustrating and destructive.

    Throughout this all, I would do everything in my power to be "me" around my kids. I refused to let them down and when I absolutely couldn't hide, I would simply tell Mark, "I can't do it," and he would understand. I would quietly go to the guest room and lie down. I would hear him telling the boys that mommy didn't feel well and for them to let me sleep. When I would wake, it was as if I had never slept. I felt heavy, nauseous, had a fever most of the time that hovered around 101 degrees. I was shaky and weak, and tears would frequently fall down my face in disgrace of myself. I didn't know what to call it or how to handle my feelings. My solution to myself when I would think of it would be to end my life. I would convince myself that the kids were better off and that they had their dad now since he had just retired from baseball. They had had enough of me and now they could have him and things would be better. I would tell myself these things in the moments of the depression, without thinking it was wrong and without hesitation. I believed in the value of this plan and began thinking of ways to execute it. When I was around the kids, I would stare at them and watch them as if it were the last time I would see them. I hadn't planned a time or date but started to believe this was my destiny.

When the depression would fade, I would have such disgust and hatred for myself, and straight-up shame. I hated that I could even think up such things and that I could do that kind of harm to my boys, my sisters, and my friends. That in itself made me feel undeserving of life. I thought about all the soldiers over in the Middle East who were losing their lives daily and here I was, taking my freedom and safety for granted. I thought about all the people and kids in hospitals fighting for their lives and here I was--wanting to intentionally end mine. I thought about my selfish thoughts and the idea of my selfishness made me hate myself even more. It was all a vicious cycle that I was dealing with every day. Fighting with every day and dying with. I never even thought these emotions could be medically related or beyond my control. I took total blame for my thoughts, my feelings, and kept thinking it was some kind of Karma I was being served. I didn't know what to do. I hid from everyone and did my best regardless for everyone else daily. As weak as I was, I refused to let on the full scope of my situation and by isolating myself it became easier to do every day.

When I finally walked into my appointment with the specialist, Dr. Shickman, it was September 10th and about 4 months since I had been bit by the tic in Central Park. I was miserable and in more pain then I had ever felt in my life. My neck was stiff, my rash was still there and I had learned to live with the daily pain of that so far. My ears hurt, my vision was distorted, I was experiencing dizzy spells, my joints were stiff, my digestion was off, I still was coughing and my energy level was nonexistent. Dr. Shickman began asking me all sorts of questions…and so I guess this takes me back to when I sat there feeling like I was on an episode of "Monsters Inside Me."

I was scared and somewhat embarrassed to be this weak in front of anyone and have to admit it! I specifically remember him asking me about the depression and if I was experiencing it or had any previous experience with it. I looked up at him when he asked me this and said "Not really." I remember the immediate lump in my throat at the thought of that question and was so beyond embarrassed to answer truthfully. I suddenly felt bad that I had lied so blatantly and changed my answer about the depression. Along with the change of answer came tears flooding down my face. I told him that I was actually feeling very depressed, more than I ever knew possible. I explained how different I felt and how out of character my attitude was, how down and I out I was and that I couldn't help how negative my thoughts were. It was then that he explained to me depression and how it's one of the many symptoms of Lyme disease and the most common one he sees in new patients. He told me that it was chemically-based and that it was nothing I could control. Once again, something in my life, adversity that I had to accept that I had no control over. I knew in this moment that even with that tiny bit of information about depression, I might not be able to *control* it, but I would be able to *take charge* of it when it arose. I began to recognize it when it came, stay calm, and see it for exactly what it was--a chemical imbalance that would soon balance out. Dr. Shickman ran quite a few other tests on me with a machine he had in his office, asked me numerous questions, and gave realistic answers to mine. He didn't try to paint pretty pictures or facades. He was direct and to the point and told me that he would need to do a series of blood tests and that in three weeks' time we would review results, prognosis and treatment if needed. In the meantime, there were obvious suspicions of Lyme disease and so to be diligent, he prescribed me an oral antibiotic and off I went to get blood pulled.

During those three weeks that I waited for my results, I contacted UCLA, even USC, as well as other hospitals with infectious disease centers. Nobody seemed able to help me and especially without a formal diagnosis. When the labs came back to Dr. Shickman, he told me that there was a definite infection and that I would need to be tested again more directly for the Lyme specifically. I was confused and upset to have to take blood again and to have waited three weeks not to even know exactly what I had. I couldn't understand why I wasn't tested for Lyme to begin with! He proceeded to tell me that my insurance didn't cover the cost of the test and that it needed to be supported by other preliminary tests. My blood would have to be drawn again and that would cost me $475.00 out-of-pocket. This would mean another three weeks of waiting and my symptoms were not improving. I was actually getting worse. When we went over my first blood tests, there were a lot of things that I didn't totally understand. What I did hear was the word, "IV's." I don't like anything that has to do with needles and was already trying to tell him that I'd prefer oral antibiotics, but he just gave me a look and I understood. I was starting to get nervous at this point and even more nervous when he told me that I was seriously ill and needed to take it seriously. I tried to be strong and somewhat tough in front of him as if I was above all this and invincible to any kind of serious illness. I didn't even know how to be sick or how to accept someone telling me that I was! All my life I had taken precautions for my health, been a "goodie-two-shoes" so to say, and was quite literally a model for fitness and good health. How could I be so sick? It infuriated me to think that all I had fought to achieve in my life was being destroyed and taken away by a damn tic!

I didn't even flinch when Dr. Shickman first mentioned Lyme disease to me. I had no clue as to what it was. I had heard about it in relation to dogs and cats but that was all. I didn't know a human could even contract this disease, nor how devastating it could be once they did. When I went back to get my blood drawn for the Lyme test itself, Dr.

Shickman had also sent orders for me to receive some iron intravenously since I was so low and I was so weak and fatigued. Iron was to be given intravenously every two weeks to try to raise my levels and to hopefully re-infuse me with energy as well. I was like a walking dead person-- barely able to stay awake…yet unable to sleep…and barely able to even pick my feet up from the floor. I was in such pain, it didn't matter at this point what he said, I was willing to do anything. I was just happy to be somewhere that someone was finally willing to help me. I had gone through the whole summer in such pain, physically, emotionally and mentally. I needed help and Dr. Shickman was the first one to offer any hope for that.

  I walked into the infusion room and there were four recliner chairs. Three were full and one was empty and apparently waiting for me. Little did I realize that this room would become my home away from home and the place where I received my biggest humbling to date. I sat down next to a petite woman named Sue who was hooked up to an IV and medication bag. Everyone in the room except for me was actually hooked up to an IV at this point. They seemed friendly enough but were all looking at the newcomer. One of the women asked me what I had, and I said I didn't know yet but that I might have Lyme disease. I was taken aback at her forwardness and felt a bit invaded at the time. Sue was sitting next to me, struggling to open the packaging of her granola bar. I could see the difficulty she was having moving and even speaking. I assumed by her movements and voice that she had Parkinson's. When we began talking a little later, she told me that she was there to be treated for Lyme disease. I had been composed up until that point. This was about the same time that Marsha, the nurse, rolled up with her cart of tourniquets, needles and things to start my IV. She began inspecting my veins. I had tears silently rolling down my face, mortified that Sue or anyone could be that crippled from Lyme disease, and picturing myself in her shoes in no time, if Lyme was what I actually had. Making things worse, I was even afraid to get poked by the needles that Marsha was about to insert into my limp arm. Overwhelmed would be the appropriate word here. Everyone in the room was supportive and compassionate. I was scared, vulnerable, and suddenly part of a new world that would change my life forever.

  I left the infusion center with a wrap around my arm where the needle had been and I would wait another two weeks to return for my second IV of iron as well as to meet with Dr. Shickman for my test results. During that time, I was to continue the oral antibiotics and hope for the best. Hope is cool, but isn't the proactive approach I am used to taking in life, so I started to do some research on infectious disease centers, but not too much specifically on Lyme. I really didn't want to see any more than what I had seen in the infusion room up close and as real as that. I wasn't prepared to take my mind down the worst-case scenarios. I was willing to face whatever I had as it came and wanted to be careful not to manifest something I didn't have. I rolled with the punches as they came and stepped up for the next one as fast as I could. I was in pain, sick and with less than 1% immune functioning to protect me from any outside threats. I knew I was in trouble and needed to be aware and defend the integrity of whatever was still strong in my body. My best asset to date has always been my attitude and my will to step up to any challenge. I would never know what a gift that was until that time in my life.

 I was home one day and received a call from a friend's dad who had heard I was sick with no firm diagnosis. He asked me what doctors I had seen and what was going on thus far with my care. I told him that I had just received my first blood tests back and that I was in pretty bad shape. I explained my symptoms and how weak I was. He told me about a place called Bio-Medical Hospital in Tijuana, Mexico, and how amazing the doctors, nurses and level of care they gave were. He said they had saved his daughter's life. I told him how difficult it was to get help and that waiting on the blood tests before I was to go back for treatment at Dr. Shickman's was going to be tough. My immune system was in bad shape and the process of getting weaker by the day was scaring me. I have always been open to contemplating situations that may seem unconventional, and this time was no different.

After getting off the phone, I quickly looked the hospital up and made the call. I was put through to a doctor who asked me to fax my blood results. Within fifteen minutes, I received a call back from the same doctor who asked if I would be able to come in for a consultation. The doctor said that I should have been admitted two weeks prior and that they could have a van come and pick me up at my house the following day so I could begin treatment immediately. I was shocked and nervous but even more excited to begin any treatment that might possibly give me some relief and aid with the issues that had already been detected in my blood.

The next day, a van showed up at 8:30 in the morning to pick me up. Mark was incredibly nervous at the idea of me going to Mexico for treatment and staying away for two full weeks as recommended. He realized that my state of health was serious, though, and waved at me from the garage as I left the driveway. About an hour and a half later and only fifteen minutes after arriving at the hospital I was already meeting with the doctor that I had spoken with over the phone and being administered an IV as well as some other shots. I remember walking into the room that would be home the next two weeks and as soon as the nurse left, falling down on the bed with my bag still over my shoulder and sobbing. I was SO scared and felt beyond alone, lost, and confused. This was my life now and I didn't understand what I had done to anyone or anything to deserve this. I was trying to wrap my head around it but I was a mess and having a breakdown. When the nurse came back, she saw my tears and hugged me, telling me that everything would be okay. She was so kind and comforting that I started to feel bad for feeling bad and tried to pull myself together. She got me all set up and said if I needed anything that she would be right down the hall. I unpacked and got my things in order and then just sat on the bed staring at the wall while fluids pumped into my weak and sore veins. I missed my boys and at least felt grateful in that moment that it was me sitting there and not them.

    Bio-Med Hospital is a small and very personal hospital. There are people from all over the world that travel there for treatment. People travel to see them in Mexico because the facility is allowed to conduct certain procedures there that aren't allowed here in the United States. There are predominantly cancer patients there that have been told by traditional doctors that there is nothing left to do for them but to go home and enjoy the little time they have left. Patients who have been given up on or denied treatments that could potentially save their lives. There are many Amish people that go there as well and even people who are there for preventative treatments. The doctors represent many nations and ethnicities and I found them all to be very knowledgeable.

    Bio-Med fed me organic breakfast, lunch and dinner and fresh vegetable juices, vitamins and broth soups in between. There was always a fresh bowl of fruit and water in the room, and the nurses and staff there were second to none. I was beyond impressed at what I saw in the two weeks I was there. People arrived in wheelchairs and walked out on their own two feet. People with throat cancer that were told they had two weeks to live, leaving after two weeks with a new hope and still alive. Everyone was pretty friendly and someone was always peeking into my room and saying hello. The patients had the choice of eating together up in the cafeteria or staying in the room depending on each person's mood or condition. It took me a couple days before I was comfortable to join the others at the table for meals but I was glad for the social connections when I finally did.

It was pretty funny to me that the first time that I sat down with the doctor at Bio-Med, she mentioned to me that my coffee would be served at 6:00 sharp each morning. I told her that I didn't drink coffee. She looked up at me over her reading glasses and simply said, "It's not optional coffee, and not the one that you drink." I just stared at her, completely oblivious and naive. She laughed a devilish laugh and said "It goes UP, not down…" and gestured a universal gesture. I laughed nervously and wanted to refuse that coffee even more so than the traditionally served coffee, but I heard what she said and didn't argue her protocol for me. My list of outlandish things I have done in my life would clearly keep expanding…and I would be taking coffee straight UP at 6:00am daily! I had never had an enema and couldn't imagine one with coffee. I wasn't a coffee drinker in the first place and suspected that after this, I would probably never be one! I will say that I was getting more comfortable with it until the male nurse came knocking one morning. I was mortified and all of the sudden I felt like I was in a Southwest Airlines commercial, and I was the perfect image to flash next to their slogan of, "Want to get away?" I played that line in my head the whole time he was in the room giving me the enema. I never even looked at him. He kept talking and asking me how I was feeling and I just lied there ignoring him and nodding a little in response so as to not be too rude. I just wanted him out of the room and out of my personal space! Of course I requested that he not be the one doing that to me again, but the nurses themselves just nodded in response, and then laughed later, I'm sure.

    It's a totally different world to live in when you are on the inside of illness. We pass by hospitals and see them off the side of the freeway, rarely taking the time to contemplate that there is a whole other world inside, lives that are at stake, and people that are teetering on the brink of living and dying. I discovered that there is a lot of compassion amongst most patients within those walls and many truly rallied and cared for one another. The vulnerability that is present in illness is compelling and I saw raw fear, tears, truth, love and humility amongst the sick as well as their healthy family members that were there with them.

 I continued to call Dr. Shikhman's office daily from Bio-Med in order to inquire about my lab results. I was finally contacted back with a positive confirmation of Lyme disease and the recommendation that I start IV's as soon as I returned. In spite of everything, I still didn't realize what this meant for me or how bad I really had it. I kept thinking of Sue and the condition I had seen her in that first day at the infusion center. I was scared but ready to accept and take charge of whatever was being dealt to me. I couldn't complain. God had answered my earlier prayers by sparing Bryce's life like I had begged for in the hospital when his heart stopped. I had made a deal to never ask for anything again. I was humbled, scared and nervous yet grateful that it was just me--and I could take this.

 I wasn't sure what to expect next or if I even had the right to expect anything at all. I was prepared to get well but I also was preparing myself for the worst. I began writing in two separate journals to my boys, talking to them about love, life, being gentlemen, what books I would recommend them to read, about myself and how I came to be their mommy. I spoke about their dad, about their grandparents, sports, heart and ego and above all else, the need to be kind. I cried at times and laughed at others as I wrote to them both. I told them of my favorite moments with each of them and how truly blessed I was to be given the opportunity to know them both. I told them that if anything happened to me that I would always live in their hearts and that my mission on this earth had been completed through them. I tried to give them strength through my words and in doing so I also felt stronger myself and ready for whatever was to come when I left the safety of Bio-Med. I closed both their journals with the simple words, "I love you always, Mommy."

    I arrived home from Bio-Med on Halloween day and I was happy to see the kids and take them trick-or-treating. My kids didn't seem to understand that I was so sick. If you're in the hospital, then you are sick. But once you are at home, standing before them, you must be well again! I was glad for their simplistic understanding of things and that they kept me focused and wanting to get better. My boys were full of demands like always and expecting me to be like I usually am on Halloween--just like one of the other kids…dressed and trick-or-treating beside them and stealing their candy along the way. I wasn't decked out in my usual G.I. Joe or Wonder Woman costume, but I did even better and dressed myself up as a healthy mom with energy. I was with Bryce and Brody until the end of the night collecting candy and jumping from behind bushes to scare them like always. I was so happy to be out of the hospital and grateful for every minute I was in their presence.

When I was told that week by Dr. Shikhman that I would need six months of IV medications and treatment, it was hard to contemplate all of the ways that my life would change. In spite of all that I have said, I truly didn't appreciate how sick I was. I thought we just needed to diagnose and treat and move forward. When I started on the IV's, I thought for sure that I would be better in half the time they had quoted me. I had always healed faster than doctors had expected with injuries, so why would this be any different! My confidence in my ability to adapt, take charge of the situation and just get better now that we knew what I was fighting against helped me for sure. But, it wasn't the answer. Lyme disease is no joke and I now know this firsthand. In spite of my original predictions, I actually spent more than double the quoted time getting IV treatments. I spent almost 14 months on IV antibiotics and at least a year and a half after that detoxing and trying to maintain some kind of functional health. It was a long and humbling road to recovery. Unfortunately, there is no final cure for Lyme disease and I still remain prone to episodes years later.

Since I have been off the daily treatments and abundance of pills, I have worked to preserve the integrity of what is healthy and strong in my body. I recognize that my immune system is better, but not perfect. I am careful not to put myself into situations that I previously thought nothing about. I remember going surfing one time last year when I apparently contracted a virus of some sort and came out of the water with swollen eyes and face and a growing red rash on my cheeks and neck. I later developed a cough that I couldn't shake for months and even developed fluid around my heart. It was awful. These kinds of things are now a part of my reality and I have to walk a careful line as I try to live life to its fullest while also trying to preserve and protect my health.

Before my Lyme diagnosis, I was riding my horse, Kid Vicious, almost every day, working intently on being able to jump him and read distances to jumps. Although this isn't an easy task, I had gotten to the point where I could take him to shows with some success. After developing Lyme and perhaps because of some of the medications, my depth perception was affected and I could no longer get a consistent read on jumps. This broke my heart.

Being on the mats through my sickness, as well as during the healing process, helped me to regain my strength both mentally as well as physically. Some people might think that doing anything where my weak, sick joints might be manipulated would be a bad idea. Even me, I thought a lot about this, jiu-jitsu itself kept me in motion on tough days when I felt like I wouldn't even be able to get out of bed. Sometimes I couldn't. But when I showed up, every pat on the back I received, every hug and gesture of good energy helped me to heal. Healing is a slow process, and unfortunately there is no rushing or controlling of something that is so much bigger than you. We need to be patient and take charge and be respectful in knowing that without health, we are nothing and we have nothing.

Chapter Nine

"TRUE BOUNDARIES"

"True boundaries are the ones we set for ourselves, not the ones others want us to set for ourselves."

-D.M.

I don't believe that I ever developed any healthy appreciation for boundaries when I was growing up. My actions were primarily governed by my own instincts, needs, and desires, and I feel as if I sort of parented myself and thought I had gotten by just-fine-thank you-very-much. Obviously, though, certain things slipped through the cracks. Children are not intended to raise themselves for good reason. When a baby is born, his or her parents begin teaching their version of what is right and what is wrong through the actions they model and the words that they use. Ideally, these teachings are achieved in a positive way- through scolding or redirecting when something is dangerous, encouraging and prodding when support is needed, and logical and appropriate consequences when mistakes are made. Through their words and actions, parents essentially start to demonstrate for a child where their personal boundaries are and what they should and should not do and perhaps more importantly what others should or should not be allowed to say or do. These boundaries, whether a parent recognizes it at the time or not, help shape or even dictate in many ways how a child grows up and handles various situations in their lifetime. From personal relations to professional, our understanding of boundaries can set the tone for our behavior, and, more critically, our expectations of others. I believe that we form these understandings early and that they help determine what we ultimately tolerate or expect in subsequent relationships in our lives.

As I entered my 30's, I began to realize that my boundaries were something I hadn't paid much attention to in life. Perhaps I hadn't needed to through the course of life thus far. I was engaging with people on even playing fields, people who were driven, positive and with common energy and attitudes. After my eternal engagement to Mark ended, I tried to keep myself open to finding love, and to finding that perfect connection with a person that I could happily spend the rest of my life with. As much as I appreciated the way that Mark and I could co-parent and raise the boys together as a slightly unconventional family, I think that his mere constant presence in my life prevented me in some ways from being comfortable embarking on a serious relationship with anyone else. As the years went by and our boys grew up, I felt that Mark took up so much space in my life--but simultaneously created an ever greater void. I suspect he could say the exact same thing about my role in his life. I don't want either of us to resent the other for this and I know that I don't regret the time I set aside to focus my heart only on my sons and I am grateful to have had Mark as my partner while I did exactly that. Whatever the reason, though, I finally arrived at a time when I felt I was lonely and ready to allow someone into my life. More importantly, someone that would be there to love me back when my boys were grown and living their own lives. It scared me sometimes to contemplate what I would have in my life if I didn't have my boys to tend to every day. I didn't want to grow old alone.

    When I think of an ideal relationship, I think of Grandpa Sam. I miss watching him with Judi. They were my model of genuine relationship and of the love that I want one day for myself. I remember asking my Grandpa how and why it was that they always seemed to get along and were so happy together. He told me that they had their share of arguments, but that the critical point was that their basic respect was never violated. He also said something so simple--as he always seemed to do: "When I make a mistake at Judi's expense, I never make the same mistake twice." I have thought about this comment many times, and have done my best in friendships and other relationships to follow his model. It's not easy, but when you love, respect, and truly care about another person, it really is that simple. I get it. I am now only wishing someone else could get it and love and treat me half as well as my grandfather loved and treated Judi.

  I tried to focus on my boys and other passions and on life goals. I had been working steadily and consistency through the belt ranks at my jiu-jitsu studio where I had also helped develop, cultivate, and teach the children's program. The jiu-jitsu studio was like a home to me and the people were like a second family. I felt safe and secure there. But, I can say now that I have never been more beat down by anyone in my life than by the person I sought out to teach me how to protect myself. I fell in love with my instructor and crossed that line and I paid dearly for it. I thought that because he had reached such a high level in an art that I regarded as precious, that he must be a wonderful human being. I was wrong. I have never met a bigger bully in all my life.

Throughout the relationship, I came to realize how weak my personal boundaries really were. Early on, there were plenty of good and passionate moments in the relationship. Quickly, though, it became a relationship based totally on control. If BigBully felt that he had control of me, all was well in the world. If not, then I paid a high price of verbal beat-downs, terrible insults, and eventually physical attacks. I used to hate myself for not being able to stand up to this person. He cheated on me, manipulated me, hurt me, and then apologized and preyed on my weaknesses. He was jealous and never supportive of my goals or willing to celebrate my accomplishments. He put me down and mocked me when I was sick, and he held me back selfishly from my professional modeling and television jobs when I was feeling strong. I was always nervous for whatever could bother or trigger him next. It was so unpredictable that there was no way to even guess what I should or shouldn't do. I would get outlandish texts from him sometimes--telling me ridiculous things like that I had "smiled too big" at someone that day. I was caught in a cycle of abuse and yet somehow I could dismiss it, explain it away, and even make excuses for him and excuses for myself. I was embarrassed for going back to him when we would break up and I eventually stopped talking to my friends about him or telling them how he treated me. I sometimes refer to these as my "isolation years." I knew enough to know my situation was very unhealthy and wrong, but perhaps on some level I didn't believe in my heart that I deserved any better. I tried to change myself so that I could be more of what I believed he wanted me to be, and when that wasn't good enough, I would search high and low for who I thought I used to be until I realized I didn't even know myself at all anymore.

  I knew that BigBully was extremely insecure. I fought for peace with him, though, and there wasn't a day- no matter how bad it got-that I didn't believe in BigBully's positives possibly outweighing his negatives. I tried to prove that to him and to myself, to believe in him, and to love and support him so much that he would love and believe in me right back. In retrospect, I think on some level that the familiar instinct to tend and befriend in times of great fear or stress was now crippling me as I tried to tend and befriend the enemy himself. To make him love me, to make him love himself, to fix him, to fix me…If I could nurture him, nurture myself, and get us through this crisis, then maybe everything would be okay. I don't give up easily on anything I want, and in this situation, I wanted to prove to him that I was worthy of love and that he could love me if he just stopped hating me and wanting to control me. The worse he treated me, the more I tried to answer back, to tend and befriend, to love him enough that he would finally love me back. It makes me sick to look back at myself and be able to so clearly explain what I was doing and why, and yet, I try to be compassionate now with myself and appreciate that I was never the one to blame and was simply never equipped with the tools to deal with someone as ugly as him.

My boundaries were nonexistent, my self-esteem was incredibly poor, and my emotions were being manipulated so much by BigBully that I eventually believed everything he said about me and therefore that I deserved everything that he did to me. I have never seen a person with so much to offer find a way to consistently give so little and take so much. This BigBully's level of carelessness and lack of compassion is ugly beyond words. It wasn't even just with me. It made him feel powerful to hurt me and then make me watch him laugh in my face while I struggled to recover. He would beat me down only to pick me up and build me up so he could start over again with me as an even weaker opponent the next time around. On top of the many complicated issues within the relationship itself, I was also constantly striving to keep peace so that I could continue my journey at the school where I had built what I believed to be lifelong friendships. I hung on so I could be granted my Black Belt alongside people I loved, trusted, and admired. I did that at a very high price that nobody truly knew the depths of. Eventually, even when BigBully and I hadn't been together in a long time, I found myself still enduring his bullying wondering if it was better or worse to walk away from him.

I have to take accountability for myself in all of this. Of course I was enabling BigBully and adding to his courage and power every single day that I stood there taking it, never mustering up the strength to fight back or even leave when I should have. I would walk away or talk back with my words plenty of times--and that would escalate and intensify the situation and usually make it increasingly dangerous the next time around. BigBully would show up at my house in the middle of the night while the boys and I were sleeping, threaten me, harm me, shame me, or simply scare me. He once gave me a concussion by attacking me in my own driveway. I have always prided myself on my strength and ability to fight and be a warrior when I need to, so it was disturbing to me that I didn't have the strength to leave or even to stand up for myself at all. For some reason, I didn't seem to love myself enough anymore to harness my resources and fight back. I also realize now that my strength of forgiveness had become my own worst enemy and that the only person I really needed to forgive was myself.

Ironically, because of the work I did as a female self-defense instructor, I had started speaking to little girls in Girl Scout troops, at school assemblies, and even in corporate forums about assault, bullying, recovery, empowerment, and even boundaries. Yet, I was caught up in an abusive relationship and was practicing none of this for myself. I felt like a true hypocrite. I kept believing in this person who obviously didn't even believe in himself. I thought he would change and evolve from this ugliness at some point into the man I believed he was or could be. I thought he would eventually prove to be high level black belt on the inside because of who the black belt he so confidently wore around his waist. BigBully is living proof that a person can achieve high levels of success in something and still never truly evolve on the inside. BigBully remained ugly and he abused his power for evil and self-serving purposes.

    This was all a great lesson that helped me realize our degrees and titles don't define us. Just because someone has a Black Belt or a respected title like President or C.E.O., those are titles and nothing more. I am not interested anymore in formal titles or degrees. More important is to know how a person makes you feel, and how a person treats you even on their worst day. For me, that is where the true character lies and where the truth of each person is demonstrated. In this instance, the rank and position of my abuser was particularly relevant, and an obstacle to my personal goals. He held me back from my promotion to Black Belt and taunted me with his ability to control me in that regard. I kept focused on my goal and was not about to walk away from all the years of hard work without the belt that I absolutely deserved wrapped tightly around my waist.

    In November of 2014, I was finally scheduled to receive my Black Belt. I spoke to BigBully and his partner and made it clear that I did not want BigBully to have anything to do with my ceremony. When the day of the belt ceremony finally came, I stood there amongst my fellow jiu-jitsu players and a handful of my close friends and family. I actually felt proud of myself for having the strength to stand there for all I had endured on and off the mats to earn my belt. I maybe even relished the thought of finally being able to look BigBully in the eye as a black belt myself-- knowing that he no longer had the power to control me or taunt me or threaten me with the belt. When time came for the honorary Black Belt to be presented to me in the traditional manner, it was BigBully that stepped into the middle of the room and began to speak to the audience about my personal journey. It was BigBully that approached me, put his hands on me, and wrapped my Black Belt around my waist. At first, I was furious, but then I wasn't sure if this was just another sign of mockery and control or a genuine gesture of truce and apology. As always with him, I was conflicted and confused, proud and humiliated, simultaneously feeling strong and weak, and at my core still truly believing that maybe things would now finally be better between us and he would at least stop being cruel and aggressive.

    Mark, the boys, and my mom were there to witness this special day, as well as some of my dearest friends. We celebrated afterwards with lunch and cupcakes and cards and gifts and I felt loved. I was proud of myself and knew that they were all proud of me as well. That night, a group of people from the jiu-jitsu studio were meeting up to celebrate the various people who had advanced through the belt ranks. BigBully and I eventually texted separately as well, and I am embarrassed to say that we ended up together that night (as what I had hoped to be friends) and we drank and celebrated separately and later as part of a larger group. And before the night was over, I was brutally attacked and punched several times in the face and then thrown from his car. BigBully had put his hands on me and hurt me numerous times before, but never had he been so violent. Perhaps he was fueled by anger that he could no longer control me by lording my black belt over my head and this compelled him to take his aggression further than ever before. Whatever the reason, I was not going to take it anymore. I called the police to report what he had done to me. Perhaps I was fueled by a strength and belief in myself after achieving something so special earlier that day. I know I felt an obligation to all the women and children I had taught how to protect and defend themselves. Whatever the reason, this would be the last time. I filed a police report and painfully shared all the details of the night.

The police went to arrest him but could not find him. BigBully was never arrested that night and not any time thereafter. As a matter of fact, to this day, essentially nothing has happened to him of any consequence. The law is strange and with many loopholes. Many times, perpetrators of "domestic violence" aren't prosecuted because the victim changes his or her mind and drops the charges. In my case, I said I would do the right thing and stand up and follow through and that is exactly what I did. Still, the San Diego District Attorney's office found that there needed to be more evidence to be able to prove beyond a reasonable doubt to twelve jurors that he did what he did to me. Without an admission of guilt or witnesses, there would be no way to convict him of a crime. I don't want to get into the many technicalities of the case or present a legal analysis. What I do want to say is that fighting to have BigBully convicted was almost certainly much harder on me than it ever was on him. I had an incredibly supportive team and a detective, sergeant, and others in the local police force that not only believed me but that fought hard to get my case to advance through the system.

The evidence that was presented was solid and the District Attorney that was originally assigned to the case was on board for prosecution. There are a lot of details that most people never heard about. People kept asking me why he hadn't been arrested initially. It wasn't until the detectives and I put things together that they realized the original 911 call was dispatched to a sheriff that actually was friends with BigBully and helped him evade arrest. This discovery prompted an internal investigation in the department that incriminated BigBully and another high-ranking professor at the jiu-jitsu studio for secretly meeting the next morning in a parking lot and plotting with the sheriff to craft a story and evade arrest and prosecution. The more I learned about this and the confidential details of the case that were shared illegally with BigBully, the more disgusted I felt to think that their ugly and illegal behaviors could ever prevail over my honest truth and innocence. I could spend time lamenting the weaknesses of our system or what a shame it is that BigBully will never have to accept criminal responsibility for what he did to me. However, I choose to let go of that. I can't take control of the system. I did my best. I took charge and I fought hard from myself by standing up and speaking out and doing the right thing. I can only control myself and my own attitude and effort, and in this case I have no doubt that I did every single thing that I could. I took charge, I finally fought back my hardest and smartest against BigBully, but I ultimately had to accept that he would never be held criminally responsible for what he did to me.

Through all of this, I continued to be blessed by the love and support of friends who helped me get through the darkness that sometimes seemed determined to collapse around me. Courtenay and Shannon sat by my side during every single court hearing and literally held my hand at times when I needed it. With their encouragement and support, I fought to protect myself from BigBully by seeking a restraining order from the courts. BigBully hired a prominent defense attorney and turned the matter into a mini-trial of sorts with experts and testimony from both sides. The judge listened to more than ten hours of testimony-- including sworn testimony from BigBully and myself-- and then issued a one-year restraining order after she commented on my credibility and determined that his testimony "didn't make sense" and was not credible. Because of continuing efforts by BigBully in the following months to intimidate me further, even with the first restraining order in place, a new hearing was later scheduled in order to extend the restraining order. Another San Diego Superior Court Judge issued a 5-year renewal of the restraining order, writing in the verdict that, "The court finds petitioner has met her burden of proof to warrant the reissuance of the R.O. based on a reasonable fear of ongoing abuse. Based on respondent's conduct and the evidence presented, it appears he has not moved on and wants to remain a presence in her life. The court grants the renewal of the R.O." The knowledge that a restraining order is in place certainly brings me some security and comfort in spite of the fact that he is allowed to walk around as an innocent man even given his illegal actions and violent disposition and history.

To truly take away every life lesson from this experience, I also need to take responsibility for my own actions and inactions that got me to the position I ended up in with BigBully. If I had boundaries in the beginning, true boundaries, and I had actually respected them, I would have never found myself in that situation. We can't rely on the law to handle all our discrepancies in life or to make justice prevail when we have been wronged or are in danger. We must stand up and protect ourselves. We must learn the value of ourselves and the need to protect ourselves with healthy boundaries. Even if we learn these late in life and through painful lessons, I like to believe that once we understand the need for these boundaries that we can protect ourselves forever after. Every person has an intuition. It's powerful and real. I made mistakes by not having clear boundaries in my life, and I paid a high price for it. I lowered my standards for myself against my better judgment and lacked the self-discipline and self-respect to remove myself from an unhealthy situation. I know I didn't ever deserve what happened to me, but I am still responsible for thinking that I could change this person--even if it was only through love and kindness.

    Boundaries are pertinent to a healthy life both personally as well as professionally. The way we choose to treat others as well as ourselves is inevitably what will define us. It takes courage to stand up for yourself. It takes courage to establish boundaries. Sometimes that means getting rid of people in our lives that are unhealthy or not in our best interests. We all have a right on this earth to live and thrive. We have a right to love and to be loved back with respect and consideration. There will always be liars, cheaters, manipulators and sociopaths and they will always have their group of minions and followers. Walk away. Trying to change these people into loving and considerate human beings will only get you hurt. Instead, learn to protect yourself and your loved ones from them. Learn to identify them and learn to walk away. Setting boundaries in life will allow you this freedom. They don't change. They are empowered by your attention, your company, and validated by who you are. Weakness is common and easy. True strength and establishing true boundaries is something for the better person and people in this world and we should all strive to achieve that.

    Being a secure person allows one to love without restriction of image and to always be kind. For me, having a Black Belt is something that I feel inside myself and if I didn't feel like I deserved it on the inside, I surely wouldn't be wearing it around my waist. It's not just about physical abilities on the mats or how many medals you've won in competition. It's much bigger than all that. It has to do with my journey of self-mastery. It has taken more than 35 years to establish my boundaries and I learned to do so the hard way. My clear boundaries will forevermore determine which people I allow in my life, allow around my children, and allow by my side. It doesn't interest me what your title is or what you've accomplished financially or professionally or physically. I care what kind of person you are and how you leave me and others feeling. It doesn't mean I think of myself as some high and mighty judge of others. It simply means that I will create the best environment for myself with healthy people that will help maximize the potential I have in this life and all that I set out to do.

I found myself distancing quite a bit from the world of jiu-jitsu after all that I went through with BigBully and the legal system. I felt alienated from the studio and quite honestly didn't want to be anywhere that he could potentially show up. Friends from the studio that I thought were true and sincere seemed to disappear overnight. I suffered losses on many levels through this, and I stopped practicing jiu-jitsu altogether for many months. It took the encouragement of complete strangers and even a few friends before I was able to step back on the mats at all. Even then, I wanted to burn the Black Belt that BigBully had put around my waist and couldn't imagine ever wearing it again.

Then, one day in the summer of 2015, the United Fighting Arts Federation (UFAF) invited me to participate in an event that they were hosting in Las Vegas. I did weapons demonstrations, spent some time getting to know some of the key people in the organization, and helped referee a couple of the matches in the tournament. I was also invited to attend an awards dinner banquet at the hotel. And so it came to be that I somehow found myself, less than one year after first earning my Black Belt, as an invited guest at an awards banquet hosted by UFAF. I was honored that night and acknowledged on stage with an honorary Black Belt degree from the UFAF. And, would you believe that I had that honor bestowed upon me by nobody other than the founder of UFAF, the legendary Mr. Chuck Norris himself.

Like so many other situations in my life, this surreal set of circumstances simply left me feeling blessed beyond words. I felt as though I had been given a chance to write a different ending to my Black Belt story. This time around, though, I earned my Black Belt from a man that I had revered and admired from afar as an example of a true "Good Guy" for as long as I could remember. I was proud to know that I had earned the respect and regard of someone that I held in such high esteem and this time I had no doubt as to whether I deserved the Black Belt. Beyond that, Courtenay and Shannon had joined me in Las Vegas for the special experience, and I was even given a second chance to celebrate the right way--surrounded by true friends that loved me, supported me, and were proud of me for me. It was a stark contrast to the night after I earned my Black Belt from BigBully and I was grateful for the almost symbolic second chance I had been given to have the Black Belt experience I deserved.

Second chances are rare in life. I wish there was a way to simply grant a certain strength and courage to everyone who needs it, so that they might be able to handle situations in a healthy manner the first time around. It would be great if people would automatically know how to handle bullies and abusers without ever hearing of, much less experiencing any pain themselves. I know that's not possible, so it has become my life mission to empower others and to share my story and what having true boundaries means to me. Protecting yourself from the inside out is important in this world. I humbly consider myself an imperfect but relatively accomplished person. I was on the cover of Sports Illustrated: Women. I have traveled the world. I have two amazing children. I have a college degree from UCLA. I have had a successful career as a model and a surfer and an athlete and in TV and film. I am a freakin' Black Belt! And in spite of all that, I didn't have any true boundaries and I suffered the consequences and became a victim instead of a warrior I am meant to be. Issues of any kind don't discriminate. Anything can happen to anyone at any time. I tried so hard to protect myself from the outside in. I accumulated accolades and honors and titles and certifications in safety and security and even a Black Belt. Ultimately, though, none of these wielded any power whatsoever in the face of a BigBully. I only discovered my true strength and power when I learned to protect myself…from the inside out.

Chapter Ten

"ENJOY THE PROCESS"

Healing is liberating. It's a gift and a blessing and it absolutely takes work. No one can heal you better then YOU. You have to be the champion of your own charity, so to say, and be proactive about it every step of the way. After more than 35 years of life, I knew I needed to take the time to heal from my Lyme disease, from the damage done by BigBully, and even from some unresolved issues from my childhood. Even the healing aspect of these parts of my life, after the worst is presumably over, has been hard on me. Recommendations and advice is abundant, and even people who haven't been through the same situations have something to say. I am happy and grateful for any love and advice and know that no matter what I expect, tomorrow will most likely be very different than today.

Hindsight always shows us things from a different perspective. How desperately I sometimes wish that we could simply listen to the wisdom of our elders and learn from their mistakes! One thing I know is that I only need to personally learn a lesson once and then I won't make the same mistake again. In order to ensure that, I have to be willing to look back at my situations and experiences and evaluate them carefully enough so that I can truly identify the core issue and learn from it and move past it. I realize first and foremost that the one thing I have perfected is the art of never giving up. I never gave in or up when I was growing up, when I battled Lyme disease, or when I finally stood up to BigBully. Keeping in forward motion and never being willing to quit kept me always moving in the right direction.

    The combination of my life experiences, talents, and passions recently inspired me to create the True Boundaries Charitable Foundation. This nonprofit foundation is a shared project with some of my close friends that helps bring awareness to assault, domestic violence, rape and anti-bullying. I know that my personal experiences in this life combined with my training in personal protection and martial arts have placed me in a unique space where I can truly hear and understand the struggles of others on their own journey. My platform is one of prevention and proactive measures, spreading awareness and understanding so that self-defense and reactionary measures are needed less often. Although I have always been open to pursuing many interests and passions that present themselves, this is truly a life mission for me and one that I am proud and excited to pursue with purpose and bring to fruition. I hope to be able to spread the True Boundaries message to anyone who will listen and for many years into the future. I like to think I have a gift to see the best in people. Their strengths and weaknesses are revealed to me in ways I can't explain and I usually know how to get in there, help them see it themselves and then encourage them to take action. Healing is something we can all do and be a part of. You don't have to be sick to be liberated by the miracle of healing. Healing in the heart and soul can be just as important for a full filled and happy life. It's important to recognize the places inside yourself and to give yourself the permission and opportunity to do the very same. I am hoping to reach out and use this book as platform to reach and speak to people that need someone to knock on that door in their lives. People that need the love and encouragement to do something and take action. People that need that little bit of encouragement to follow their passions and to chase their dreams. Give yourself the permission to do so and you'll be surprised at what you're truly capable of.

So many things play a role in recovery from any illness or trauma, but none of those things are going to work without the attitude being in the right place at all times. I am not going to lie and say that I woke up every day with an amazing attitude, because surely I did not! I had plenty of days where I wondered if it would be my last and days in a deep depression when I even thought of taking my own life. Instead of ignoring or trying to forget these memories and emotions, I try to harness them now and learn from them and use them to help me understand and guide anyone else who finds themselves feeling the sense of despair or disillusion I have experienced in my own life. I am particularly passionate about taking every opportunity I can to touch the life of a child who needs it. I remember so many great individuals who touched my life for the better and maybe never knew the positive impact they had…coaches, parents, friends, and even complete strangers, like the kind lady who opened the bathroom for me every morning so I could clean up at the beach before school. These memories of amazing people in my own childhood will always motivate me to be a positive guiding force in the lives of children any chance I get.

When I was younger, I remember coaches in virtually every sport who would stand in front of the team and tell the kids that they wanted to see 100% out of them every single time they took the field. I would always think to myself that it's impossible to be 100% every single day and in every circumstance. I remember having the feeling that I wasn't good enough a lot of the time because of this. No matter how much I would give on some days, I couldn't give 100% of my potential to every single activity on every single day. No one else will ever know the pressures exerted on certain people. Teenage girls are maybe starting their periods and beginning to deal with hormonal changes. Some kids have great homes they can retreat to, and maybe some don't have homes at all. Relationship issues with parents, boyfriends, girlfriends, school and work struggles, injuries, or maybe someone just not feeling well…these are all legitimate issues that will lead to variability in performance. Showing up with 100% of our potential every single day just isn't realistic. If pressured to do so, kids and even adults can begin to feel insecure about their abilities and eventually, themselves.

When I coach kids or conduct seminars at schools, I tell the kids that I realize that life is happening to you before you ever show up and that some of you might not have things orderly and great at home, school, or other areas of life. I know that you all come out here to do your best with intention on giving your best as well. Of course I would love to see 100% out of every one of you, but I know this isn't realistic...So, I want you to be honest and ask yourself what percentage you are at every day. Are you 100%? Are you 80%? Are you 40%? Which is it? Maybe you're 10%? I don't know this, and only you will know this for yourself. Whatever it is, I'd like you to declare that percentage to yourself, and when you're out here or wherever you are in life, insist on giving 100% of that number to yourself--as well as to me or your coach. Be okay with where you are and accept it. Feel good about it and own it. Once I've declared that number to myself no matter how low or high it is, I almost always supersede it throughout the day. Being 100% or in the "zone" is a special place. We aren't entitled to it. It takes work, strategy and skill to stay in it once you get there. If everyone knew how to be 100% every day, there would be no extraordinary humans out there, everyone would be perfect. My new 100% is more like my old 80%. Since being diagnosed with Lyme, I'm usually around

80%, but I can assure you I get 100% of wherever I'm at each day! It's okay and it's called being human.

    I have watched kids completely transform in front of my eyes with this approach. I have seen their confidence shine on and off the field and actually become way more than what they even declared that had the potential for initially. This approach to kids, or anyone, is something I have found to be real and very powerful. It is exactly what I would tell myself every day when I was sick with Lyme disease. There were even some days that I would literally declare that I had only 1%. Instead of them asking me how I was feeling and me saying, "Awful," which was how I felt most of the time, I would say, "I'm about 5% today." Simple. I accepted where I was, but I didn't make excuses for what I could do or what I could not do. I relieved any pressure on myself and allowed my body to have the opportunity to heal at whatever pace it was going to heal at. Whatever I had was enough. I was enough.

    I wake up every day and check myself. What percentage am I today? You had better believe I will take 100% of whatever it is. There are many different aspects of healing. There is physical healing, emotional healing, and even mental healing. I have a few people that I have leaned on a lot, whether they know it or not, to help with my healing. My friends have been so amazing through this, and my words could never give them justice or the thanks they deserve. I am not good at talking about my own problems with other people. I have always been more of the rock to my family and friends. I am awesome at navigating other people's problems-much better than I can navigate my own. I am amazing at protecting and standing up for my friends, even a stranger, but have come to learn that I am terrible at doing the same for myself. I can picture so many instances where I would be on the phone with family or friends, helping them deal with their issues, while I was battling my own issues that they knew nothing about. However, this process would truly help me to stay strong in some ways. My eternal instinct to tend and befriend others would give me a motivation to stay strong myself so that I could keep at it and be that rock to everyone I cared about. It has always been easy for me to be strong for others, but very difficult to do the same for myself.

  I remember that my friend Lindsey drove by my house when I wasn't there one day and left a little note card and some flowers on my bed. The note said, "You are loved so much! Feel better!" She will never know how far that went and how powerful that was for me. I taped that note to my bed and saw it every day. My friend, Quentin, would text me daily right around 1pm before my IV and send good energy and love. People would call at random times and say the most amazing things or even the simplest things that would push me through the toughest moments with Lyme disease or other dramas and challenges. I write this right now and am in awe when I pause to think about all the wonderful people I have in my life and how much strength and love they have given me. Who am I to deserve this? Seriously. I am just blessed, because nothing else could explain it. As I have said before, I have extraordinary people in my life, simply extraordinary. I feel like a magnet for them. I laugh about this, but it's true. I am the weakest link amongst these people and am only here because of their love and support. Each one of them has supported me and carried me in their own way and I am forever grateful for the strength given to me in those tough moments that have carried me through.

    Unless you really know me, you would never assume how sensitive I really am. I look strong and probably pretty tough on the outside, but I am the complete opposite on the inside. Even my friends have been surprised by my sensitivity and my difficulty dealing with things when it comes to matters of the heart. As I said before, I give great advice from the outside in these situations but can't save my own life when it comes to issues for me. I am so soft that I actually get mad at myself. There is nothing more disturbing for me than a broken heart or confrontation or aggravation with a loved one. I can't function, eat, sleep, or do anything. It sucks my energy dry and deflates me in a way only that issue can. It overcomes me and I have always been perplexed at how Courtenay and other girlfriends can stay so strong when dealing with the same. No matter how hard I have tried, I could never seem to rectify this. Only now am I finally starting to get a grip on this. I simply couldn't take it anymore being that way within myself. This healing process has opened my eyes to the best and worst in people, shown me who my real friends are, and revealed my character even more to myself.

    The healing process with my Lyme disease and BigBully have helped me to get a grip on my emotions as well as my emotional needs. Being sick exposes a lot more than just your physical weaknesses. It exposes your abilities as well as your worst and best qualities. All adversity, sickness or even heartbreak is humbling. Heck, an arm bar is humbling. In jiu-jitsu, you make mistakes that other people have the opportunity of capitalizing on. Either way, whether you are tapping out or submitting someone else, you are learning-and somewhere in that process is the gift of humility.

Throughout my healing process, I have read books, a lot of books, and many of them at once sometimes. I will pick a book up off the stack I have beside my bed and just read. It seems that somehow, I will always turn to the page and find exactly what I need to read that day. I find that reading positive things or books about adversity and love are helpful. I like reading other people's stories about their triumphs and tribulations no matter what they are. Reading about human frailty and people who fight for what they believe in is compelling. Reading about these things releases certain endorphins into your system and can help your body to heal while you sleep or give you a better feeling during your day. Anything contributing to a positive attitude when you are sick, struggling, or upset can help me. Good movies are also great and anything or anyone that can make me laugh is also a plus.

One of the main things I have tried to change in my life for good is my relationship with stress. I have an amazing friend who has dealt with enormous stress in life, and in his speeches he claims that, "stress is a choice." I had to sit with this concept for a while. As we know, there are many different kinds of stress and each one with different consequences to the mind, body and spirit. I took what he said and tried to apply it to my life. Whenever I felt stress come upon me in any way, I thought in that moment, "Stress is a choice" and then sat with that. It is a choice in some fashions of the form. Stress sneaks up on us or can be crashed into our faces. It can be light or extreme. Stressful situations are there, whether we like it or not. The "choice" so to say, comes with how we choose to deal with those stressors once they are upon us. It goes back to attitude, not panicking and being mindful of the situation and its components. I am better prepared now for stress as opposed to freaked out or fearful of it. Stress has become something of a new challenge to myself and as I practice exerting choice in the matter, the better I get at taking charge and the better off I am- both mentally and physically.

I am excited to wake up almost every day--even when there doesn't seem to be a lot going on. I get up and am grateful to walk and move, even though I have still never regained the pleasure of getting out of bed without feeling any pain. I am at best performing at an average of about 80% nowadays relative to how I used to be. It's my new reality. But, I commit to take 100% of that number every day.

Horses have an incredible healing ability. They compensate when they are injured or sick and have hearts the size of the ocean. They are angels in fur coats and are sensitive to the emotions of their owners. Owning my own horse was always a dream of mine, and something I had wanted all my life. My horse, Kid Vicious, was a support to me and a motivating force in my healing. My relationship with this beautiful creature kept me strong on certain days and the thought of him helped me get out of bed some days. He makes me laugh, and the people I share this special space with at the barn have all encouraged and supported me tremendously. Their understanding at times when I needed it has been more then I could ask for and the care they showed Kid in my absence was a true act of kindness. Kid is a cocky horse, full of himself and tough. He has a heart of gold on the flip side and became nervous with me when I became ill. There were days when I would ride him and we would take a walk around the property on the trails that I would feel his compassion and his love. I have to say,

I love this horse! I sometimes have felt scared for how much I love him and for how emotional I have gotten just speaking about him in my life. Horses are strong animals, yet sensitive and compelled by energy-whether it be good or bad. I have had this creature since he was a baby. I know I will never ride at his level but I can't say I didn't try. I have been in awe of his wit, his talent and his will to win and be great. He is a true competitor and athlete. He wants to do everything right and perfect and when you aren't quite as perfect as him, he'll let you know and bare his frustration with a question. I always knew I wanted a horse but never realized I would love it so deeply. Kid has been a big contributor to my healing process even though I know he has no clue of that.

  Today, I am busy with life as usual for me. Unusual for most, but usual for me. I stay outside the box as much as possible and try to stuff as much into a day as possible. When people ask me what I do, my answer is staggered with activities and job titles that definitely don't belong together. My boys remain my biggest job in life and also my most rewarding privilege. I am a survivor of Lyme, a survivor in life and blessed with the most wonderful people I could ask for around me. I am healthy enough to do jiu-jitsu most days, and to share it with kids and empower others. I am compelled by my adversities to help others and to empower people with the encouragement to seek the strength in themselves they might not know exists.

After four years of retirement and spending time to bond with the kids, helping out with their baseball and so forth, Mark is back coaching in the MLB and the minor league systems. He's a great coach and a good leader. I always tell him, "You played in the MLB for 15 years! People want to know how you did that, what it took…share with them and teach them!" He's very humble and forgets what he's done sometimes and how accomplished he is. I remind him from time to time that the kids and I remain his biggest fans. The baseball life is tough on family and the kids and Mark have missed out on a lot of each other over the years. That leaves me here to guide them best I can on all fronts. I try to be the best coach I can, best influence, best comfort and security for them. It's intimidating raising two boys on my own, protecting them from the world and making sure they are happy and staying on all the right paths, giving them the best chance I can to succeed. I am very hands-on and involved with them aside from my own work and crazy schedule that still never works out on paper. It's all worth it and I'd never change a thing. One day, I'll blink and they'll be leaving for college. They are both the most amazing things that have ever happened to me.

In the course of writing my life story, I have discovered that there may never be a logical end to some of my chapters. I certainly thought at this point in life that my childhood chapter was closed and that there would be no new information for me to absorb so many years later. I have done my best to come to terms with my father's choices in my childhood and the impact these had on my life. However, I was recently blindsided by the discovery of a half-sister whom he fathered with another woman just 11 months before Karlee was born. Having someone seek Sadie, Karlee and me out and identify herself as our blood sister stirred up any number of memories and emotions and made me further question my ability to respect my own father. I don't know all the details and I am sure there are many sides to all this as I have heard from her and even Gini who whole-heartedly dealt with this. This girl's mother passed away when she was a teenager and she was left to fend for herself. Gini tells me that she and my dad paid child support to the state because her mother wouldn't allow Gini or my dad to be in her life. I have heard different accounts of this situation since she reached out to my sisters and me. No matter what the details or truth are, she didn't ever deserve to feel for all these years that she was unwanted and unloved. I know the burden is not mine to carry, but I do feel heavy knowing that another girl, my own little sister, was left to fend for herself at an age when children should be loved and protected by their families no matter what. The fact that I can still be forced to reevaluate an entire chapter of my life so many years later makes me appreciate the fluid nature and uncertainty of life. I had two sisters all my life. That WAS true. I now know I have actually had three little sisters for most of my life. That is my new truth. Life is always evolving and changing and I have to recognize that maybe there is no end to any chapter, not even one I thought had been written and closed decades earlier.

My mom today is strong. She's an amazing Grandma and my kids adore her. She helps me so much and I am so grateful for her. I see her now and after watching what she's gone through, I can honestly say I am so proud of her. She fights and is grateful. She has humility and this is one of her most beautiful assets. I love the confidence she walks with, and I know that it comes from a real and deep place. She has self-worth, she has pride, and she is compelling. I am relieved that she has found this love in her heart and is able to share it, enjoy it and continue moving forward in this world. She deserves so much and I wish her all the joy and peace she can find. Guilt is a heavy burden and I couldn't imagine bearing the weight of it. It is especially hard watching someone suffer and beat themselves up over something that they never truly knew to avoid. I believe that she was victim to her environment and her own childhood circumstances and I understand her choices as best I can. I know she is destined for wonderful things to come and I am so grateful to have been able to help her when I could along the way. I was never dealt anything I couldn't handle in this life. Even when I thought I couldn't, somehow I did. My mom was one of the most difficult situations I ever had to deal with in my youth because I longed for nothing more than to have her as my mother and not in my life today.

I am grateful to be back to work on horses. Each and every one never fails to teach me something and help me to be better for the next. I do poster restoration and body work on horses. I always felt that horses helped me heal my emotional damage when I was young. I would escape to the stables and just hang with horses, feeding them grass and chilling outside their stalls. I have always been enamored with them. They melt my heart and have the biggest hearts on the planet. I have been called in my life to give back to them and to help them even half of what they have done and given to me. Dino, an amazing human being and mentor, took me under his wing and shared his craft with me years ago. He taught me a craft that I will continue to use to help horses as long as I can walk. He is a true genius and has the heart of a warrior as well. His mission to help heal horses has inspired me and has also been a healing factor in my own life. With every horse I put my hands on and give back his/her tools, I know that I am making a life a little better and this feels good. Working on horses is taxing physically and a lot of work. It has motivated me to move through the pain I suffer on my own. Horses are incredibly determined to do their best, it's in their nature, and one of the many things that makes them so special. They have been a constant example for me of the power of heart and compensation. They always find a way and because of this, so have I. They are the epitome of giving 100% of whatever they have at the moment. I love them for this and for reasons words couldn't give justice to. Working in stalls with these creatures is my breath of fresh air and I feel privileged to do so.

One of my continued passions is the entertainment industry. As tough as it is, I absolutely love putting an unharnessed energy into something and seeing where it will go. I loved hosting sports shows and completely love the work it takes to perform in film. I love complex, dramatic characters as well as comedic roles. I am not sure where this passion factors in to my future, but I can only say that I am open to any potential and I will continue to watch for opportunity and maximize it. I've come close to booking some big and significant projects but close doesn't count in that business.

I absolutely love teaching and speaking to kids about martial arts and the benefits of it mentally, physically and emotionally. Having the opportunity to share jiu-jitsu with someone for the first time or sharing the power and efficiency of it with kids is one of the greatest things. To know that you are influencing and giving tools to a child that may save his or her life is amazing and powerful. I have had the opportunity to instruct kids and to coach them while they competed. Martial arts allow kids to gain self-respect and to understand the strengths mentally and physically like no other activity or sport on earth. To have a hand in this and to be able to touch a life or to change it altogether for the better is why we are here on earth. It's not about the belt you have around your waist or how many stripes you have on that belt. It's teaching them about life so that someday they will put the two parallels together themselves and hopefully make better decisions.

I am determined to live in the moment as much as I can each day. Actually doing this takes work. I am determined to live as long as I can for my kids and to maximize the potential of my time with them and the lessons or special things I can share with them and also learn from them. They have been such a support for me whether it's the Lyme or even my more recent back surgery. They always pick me up in all ways when I've been down. I feel like I know what I'm doing with my life right now, but that won't always be the case. In jiu-jitsu, when the instructors are showing us positions, there is always that "what if…" question thought running through your head based off of different scenarios or positions. In life, it's the same. Commit to the decisions you make and see where they take you. If you are sick, accept it and no matter what you have available that day, take 100% of it. Love with all your heart and don't let ego distort your vision of divert your decision-making from what is right and more importantly, what is real. Life is short and it's fragile. We are here for a blink in the scheme of things. At the end of the day, the people around you and your loved ones are who define you and what matters to you. Recognize this in yourself and be a hero to your own heart, to your kids and to your friends. You have that choice and tomorrow could be too late.

Be inspired by the fact the fact that you are living. Try to stop focusing on what you don't have and take a simple look at what you do have. There are people in wheelchairs who would give anything to get up and walk to the bathroom or to stand and brush their teeth. Simple things. We get so side-tracked by life sometimes and blinded to the simplicities in life. We get pulled by the daily obligations and forget what makes our hearts feel alive and beat faster or harder. Never lose sight of what makes you smile or what propels you to your personal next level. Be aware that you have passions and skills that someone else doesn't. It's what makes us all different and special. Set goals and set your mind to accomplishing them within a certain time period. Stay accountable to them and to yourself. Do something daily that gets you closer to that goal.

Put that energy and those thoughts out into the universe and you'll be so wonderfully surprised by what comes back. You are worth it and when you believe this, others will also begin to believe the same. Beyond that, by believing in yourself, you automatically give others the permission to also believe in themselves. It's a natural, positive effect and wonderful when you take notice that you are and can make positive influences in the life of another.

    Life is short and its fragile. The sooner you realize this, the more you will take each moment for what it is and make the most of it. I know how dark life can be at times, I really do. I have been devastated by all kinds of matters and situations that have left me begging for mercy, even contemplating my life as I know it. It can get scary and bad sometimes. We must believe that there is light even when we cannot see it. The more you focus and train this thought into your head, the more you will know it exists and that glimmer of hope and faith will guide you through that common darkness when it encroaches. Have that faith! Faith in yourself, in the people that you choose to surround yourself with and in all you believe in.

    Be your passion, and in turn, allow others to be inspired by you and to live beside you, compelled by your enthusiasm to thrive and to love. We all have passions--as different as they may be. Share yours with the world. Don't get caught up in how many "likes" you get on your social media sites, just be you and by doing that, you are serving the world in your own way as you were meant to. My passions are unique to me. Not everyone will want to do a martial art or roll around on the floor getting their arms cranked or even choked. I love martial arts, it's a platform that has inspired me to see life from a different perspective. Not everyone wants to be out in the ocean, catching waves or even being held down by them. I found my confidence in the ocean at a young age and it has brought me peace in some of my worst times. These passions of mine, along with others, are things in life that I believe in and find value in. They parallel my personality and I am compelled by them. They have helped me to see what I am here to do. Restoring confidence, trust and faith into children and people of all ages is beyond rewarding. When you are clear, amazing things are possible. We all have purpose, find yours and your life will change. Believe, love, share and above all, be kind. Like my Grandfather always told me and even wrote to Bryce in his inspiring letter, through being kind comes joy, love, friendship, and neither can live without the other.

I will continue on my journey to share my message of what matters most to me, and to share and bare my soul and be the best mother I can always be for my boys. I am looking forward to taking life one moment at a time and absorbing all I can from the amazing people that are in my life. I am also grateful and humbled by them all. I stay open and give thanks to all I believe in. I give thanks to God and give gratitude for being able to be a mother and for the life I live with these boys. To have the influence I have at home, out in the water, on the mats, the baseball field and even just tucking them in at night is such a privilege I'll never disregard. I give thanks for my health every day and hope that it continues to stay above water. Thank you for the time you have taken to read my story and to share in leaving this world better than when we came into it. God bless our soldiers and the people who serve this country and have given the ultimate sacrifice, your hearts are huge. For those we have lost, may your souls rest in peace.

GRANDPA SAM'S LETTER

I owe a HUGE part of who I am and who I have chosen to be to my Grandpa Sam. His kindness and huge heart inspired me to be who I am today. To make no excuses and to always keep pushing to be better. As humans, we are capable of great things. We have so much power to do more and be more then we allow ourselves on a regular basis. I am so humbled by my Grandfather and all that he accomplished in the short time he was here. He passed away in his sleep at 72 and I can assure you, he wasn't ready to go. Anything can happen to anyone of us on any day, at any time.

I will emulate his work ethic and the selflessness he demonstrated in his love for Judi and me. When I have struggled over the years, I have often spoken out loud to him, hoping to receive an answer of some kind, any kind. He was my literal and physical warm hug when I needed one and the trusted voice of reason that I could count on. He had a way of speaking to me and reaching the very depths of my being in such a way that I felt loved and understood.

My Grandfather wrote this letter to my oldest son Bryce for Christmas. I read this at his funeral and have made over

100 copies for people throughout the years. May this letter bring you insight, knowledge and a smile. It was written by one of the most angelic men to have walked this planet. He was my example of how a man should love and treat his woman. He loved people and had so much compassion for the under dogs. He also happened to love and believe in me more than anyone else in my whole life.

God bless you Grandpa Sam, may you rest in peace

Dear Bryce,

Well, it's Christmas time 2004 and you're just starting out on your life's journey; it's a tough world you're facing and you have so many adventures ahead of you. It would take days to count them even if you were an excellent counter like me. But there are rules for adventures, so I baked these cookies for your Mom and Dad to keep them busy while you and I talk about some of them; tell them they're best if eaten with ice cold milk. Now, here are some of the rules, your Dad knows them too, so always ask him if you're ever in doubt.

<u>First</u>, Ask questions; look at everything…turn over a stone and be curious about the world that lies beneath it;

smell a flower and marvel at its beauty and wonder what could create such magnificence. Feel a breeze and know it has traveled the world just to arrive at the very moment you breathe it in and take from it its life's force. These things don't happen by accident. There's a great power in the universe and you will wonder about it all your life; embrace it, question it, share it very carefully, but never doubt that it exists.

Second, Be kind, for from kindness comes friendship, trust, joy and love-each one an extension of the other. In any order, neither can live without the other; only together can they make you a whole person.

Third, Learn the value of silence because only during silence do we learn to appreciate great music, great books, great art and education. From these you will form certain judgements and opinions. Always stand firm on these and know they come from true facts, not rumors or hearsay be it about politics or a friend.

Fourth, Love. Now there's a tough one, there are many many different kinds of love-from "I love pizza" to "I love you darling" and many years will pass before you will come to understand and truly know what it is. You will love your Mom and Dad with all their faults and what you perceive as their lack of understanding of the most important thing in your life at that moment.

<u>Fifth,</u> Always have a dog in your life, for a dog expresses love like no other animal on earth. It expects nothing and appreciates everything; it will express happiness and act the fool without the restriction of image. Take a lesson from a dog and never lose the freedom to be silly; in short, never trust a man who doesn't have a dog in his life, for his world centers around himself.

Your heart will be broken many times but it will heal only to be broken again and you will learn from each until one day you meet someone who you will know is different than all the others, who will love you with all your warts, in whose company you can be comfortably drowsy knowing full well you will be together when you awake. You must always tell the truth and be where you say you will be, it will keep your heart light and you will be fearless in the face of anything.

I regret that you and I will never have time to sit down over a beer and speak of "cabbages and kings," but your Dad will handle that. Enough of the heavy stuff and we only scratched the surface. The teddy bear is probably one of many in the den, but he is the only one from your

"Great Grandpa" who will always love you. The hat is for when you go to Tibet in search of "the true meaning of life." Right now, do a big poo for Mommy, because that's your job.

Sleep well little friend,

I love you

Grandpa Sam

December 18th, 2004

Merry Christmas

ACKNOWLEDGMENTS

"No duty is more urgent then that of returning thanks."
-James Allen

In life, whether we are humble enough to see it or not, there are many people, places and things that come into our lives at the time they are supposed to and even leave our lives at the time they are supposed to. Life is full of lessons and people both good and bad, who assist us in shaping and creating who we are, in the space we occupy on this earth. We are human and that means we all have issues that are revealed to us along this journey of life. Without the special, extraordinary people I've come across, my issues never would have come to surface, allowing for my personal growth and evolvement.

I had the privilege of growing up in the best of two worlds with biological parents as well as adopted ones, all of whom taught me different lessons and values. I have also had the privilege of working all over the place with many different kinds of people, mostly extreme ones, and being a part of their everyday excellence and hard work. I have always been an opportunist, never dismissing anything before I took a look at it first. If at any time in your life you've ever been in survival mode, you will automatically become this without even recognizing that you do it. When opportunity arises, you look, listen and act. I always did so and because of this, I've been blessed with experiences that seem unreal to most people in my short life so far.

I have listened to life, tasted it, felt it, seen it and been molded into my individual self by it through one humbling at a time. Great strength can only come from true adversity and for each person, the level of that is different. Most of mine has been extreme. I am incredibly passionate about my life, the people I surround myself with and how I choose to spend my time while living. This way of life isn't for everyone and many people in my life have come and painfully gone for some of these reasons.

Acknowledging the people in my life that have helped me in one way or another either through their love or the pain they've caused me is important. Not enough times in this world do we take the time to express our gratitude to those individuals. Appreciation of things and people is something that we must never forget. One of the most rewarding things you can do is tell a person what they mean to you. Life is sneaky sometimes and that person that you were thinking about or wanted to say something to, might not be there tomorrow. Stop being too proud or too busy, text it or pick up the phone and say "Hey, I just wanted you to know that I love you!" Or, "I just wanted you to know I appreciate you…" Any of these will work and will make someone's day.

I'd like to thank my dad and mom for deciding to have me. I realize for the most part that you were both kids when you had me and had to grow up pretty fast because of me. I am grateful for that. As a mother now, I know how incredibly hard it is to have a baby to feed and care for, and the time it takes from your own lives to raise that child. I know I was born a handful and I appreciate the patience and efforts it took keeping me contained while you could.

I'd like to thank my Grandparents, Grandpa Sam, Grandma Barbara, Papa, Judi, Grandpa Andi, and my Great Grandparents, Mimi, Papa, and Noni. I have fond memories of you all, you made such valiant efforts to be part of my and my sister's lives. Grandparents are gifts, their knowledge is priceless. They are from the olden days compared to our generation. They have homegrown values that today are mostly forgotten or ignored. Men were gentleman, opening doors for women or standing up at the table when a woman approached or left. They are our last true role models and I thank God every day for each moment I spent with them. They were my example of what I hope to have in my life in terms of love, the very most important thing we will ever do. It seems that the most important things in life are the first ones we forget about and leave to always do "later." We should wisely remember that we aren't promised later, no one is.

    My family, Mark, Bryce and Brody,...

Mark, I have always been inspired by you to aim for the top and to believe that I can be or do anything. It was my honor to walk beside you and a lot behind you as you lived your dream and every other little boy's dream as a Major League Baseball player. I grew up loving the game, playing the game and grasping the specialness of it. To see the ins and outs of it and to be able to support you and live it with you was amazing. We share memories that will belong to us forever. I am excited for you and for the next chapter of your life with coaching and whatever else you choose. Never forget who you are and what you have accomplished. We fall in life, it's how we get up that defines us. You are an incredible human, never forget that. Also, never forget that you have two little guys looking up to and trying their hardest to follow in your footsteps. They need you now and will always seek your love and support. Thank you for the love, friendship, and parenting support. Our adversity as a couple crushed me but it also taught me to love you more and to accept the fact that we are only human and need to rise above ourselves for the greater of the whole.

Bryce and Brody, my princes. The depth of love I have for you both is paralyzing at times. I am brought to tears even thinking about it. Thank you for the education you have given me as a parent, a person and a woman. I am in awe of you both and excited to see what you will be one day. I try my hardest to love you with actions and pray that you don't judge me too hard for my downfalls. I will love you both unconditionally to the day I die and there is nothing on this earth I believe in more than the two of you. I promise to always be a positive presence in your lives and to guide you with all the strength in my heart. Thank you for inspiring me to be a better person every day. I hope for years and years of more memories with you both. Nothing on this earth makes me happier and more proud than the two of you.

Sadie, my sister, I love you so much and am so proud of you. You set your sights on something and go get it without question, hesitation, or excuse. You charge this life with persistence and unwavering force. Thank you for all our naughty memories of tormenting the neighborhoods we lived in and being equivalent to four little boys! We never let up when it came to playing, surfing and even fighting when it happened. I am sorry for having to leave you when I left to pursue my life amid differences with dad. I hope you know deep in your heart that I never wanted to leave you and Karlee. You were both my motivation to aim high for my goals and to never let up because I knew you two were watching. Congratulations on becoming a great doctor, I love that you love what you do, making a special difference in this world matters and you do it every day. I love you so much and am so grateful for how amazing you are to the boys. You are forever their Tia. Thank you for loving them and for helping me when I have needed it with them. They are better because of you, and so am I.

Karlee, my baby. I remember feeling you kicking in Gini's tummy and anxiously awaiting your arrival. I remember running through the halls at the hospital thinking that I was going to be able to hold you. When we got to the nursery and they shut me down, I was so upset and threw a fit. From the moment I laid eyes on you, you were mine. I remember the day you took your first steps. You have always been beautiful beyond words and I have always been in awe of your huge heart, your work ethic and the kind and hardworking mother you have become. I love you so much and wish we lived closer so I could be there to protect and love on you more. I am always right here for you. Keep aiming high and don't let the bumps along the road of life deter you from your happiness or sanity. You have so much power and purpose, stay strong. Those two little ones of yours melt my heart and they know how much Auntie Dani loves them. I miss you all every day. Time with you all is so precious. Thank you for being one of my motivations to push myself and to rise above so much adversity. Your love kept me going in some of my darkest times. Times you will never even know what you did for me. I love you.

  John and Diane, my saviors and blessings. Thank you for carrying me through the last years of high school, for all your mandatory visits to the principal's office on my behalf and for the love you showed me in your home. I can't imagine my life without the two of you. I am sorry for the distance we have now, I think of you two and wish we were close like before. I realize that life moves on and that what is not nurtured will not flourish. My love, admiration, and respect for you lives on strong and my values have been influenced by you, your family and even family friends. I thank you for all you have done for me and for making me apart of something so sacred as your family. I love you like my own parents and wouldn't be where I am without you both.

I would like to thank the friends in my life who have become family to me...I am no one without you. I have friends all over the world, they are all intense, passionate, innovative, extraordinary people who have guided me, supported me, loved me and been there when I was down and also when I was on top of the world.

Jeff, I have so much love and respect for you even though you're a Trojan! If not for you, I would never have ended up going to UCLA. It was you who kept me focused, strong and on my feet in my late teenage years. Working with you on Planet X, traveling with you, sharing time with your amazing parents and having you by my side even to visit my mom behind bars was beyond anything I could ask for in a friend. You are the epitome of patient, kind and hard working. I am and will aways be so grateful for you. You always believed in me more than I believed in myself during that time. My Grandpa loved you very much and always appreciated you having my back so much.

QC-55, Thank you for the unconditional love and support all these years. I will never forget the day I met you. You have been a source of trust and love for me, and someone I have always looked forward to seeing and spending time with. Thank for the unwavering support while I was sick and on IV's, your texts are something I looked forward to receiving on those days that seemed like my last at times. I am so grateful, after all these years to have you in my life.

Nicole M., my tall and beautiful friend and neighbor. You are brave, brilliant, and fierce. You showed me strength in ways I hadn't seen before. Thank you for being such a caring and consistent friend all these years. You inspired me to be the best mom I can be and even a better friend.

Joelie, you are nothing short of amazing and resilient in the face of anything and everything. Thank you for bringing me into your world and brotherhood. I have always loved how loyal and strong you are--standing for your friends without hesitation. We remain on the same page about many things and I love you dearly for all the times and years you have had my back. I am proud of you with all your success and I hope for many more years of friendship with you. Keep kicking ass Joelie, it's what we do!

Rudy R., my warrior twin. You are hands-down the most unique man on this planet. True to your heart and emotions at all times. Your energy and power of enthusiasm is unmatched. Thank you for your love, passion, support and friendship all these years. I am always happy to see you and share tears or smiles. I am always here for you, the good, the bad, I'll take it and be there. I love you Rudy, stay strong and keep spreading your light.

Anthony A., one of my most loyal of friends. A beast, a real man and someone I know I can call on and will be there front and center willing to do anything for me. Thank you for reaching out to me in one of my darkest times and lifting me up. You were a complete stranger and you messaged me on FB to pick me up out of nowhere. I will never forget your thoughtfulness and kindness. I was going through one of the worst times in my life and you came from nowhere and helped me back to my feet. I will always believe there is good in this world despite all the rotten things that can happen because of people like you! You are a true brother. I am blessed to know you. You messaged me daily, reminding me that I wasn't alone and to stay strong. Words don't describe what that did for me.

To the girls, my teammates at UCLA, my Bruin Family, you changed my life and own a huge piece of my heart forever. Thank God for Facebook and for the BruinBandwagon!! Sue, Kelly and Lisa, thank you for believing in me and for allowing me to be part of something bigger than myself. Thank you for allowing me the opportunity for an amazing education and for an experience I never thought was possible for me. I am eternally grateful and bleed blue and gold forever. I love you all and cherish the rich memories that could never be compared or replaced. I am a better, stronger and more grateful woman for ever having known you. Kirk, you are also a huge part of that. I will always be someone you can count on to show up for you all and give and do what I can. Thank you for everything!

Thank you all my coaches in sports both good and bad who saw the best in men and pressed me to bring it out. To those of you who pulled me aside to say a few words that changed a perspective or my attitude at the time, you matter. Bob Curtis, you taught me about God, patience and to believe in my abilities no matter what happened. To have faith in God and myself and to always do the right thing. Thank you to my acting coaches, Steven Anderson and Tom Ardavany. Steven, thank you for teaching me the importance of the moment. Staying present isn't as easy as it sounds. Thank you to all the people out in the water from the time I was 7 until now who pushed me into waves or hooted me into them, encouraging me to be the best I could. Lyle, thank you for paddling out to Waimea with me and for helping me to make my dream come alive by dropping into 20 foot waves. There is nothing like it and I will never forget it! Thank you Sue Enquist for taking a chance with me and for allowing me to be apart of the greatest sisterhood in the world. I wear that badge and those four letters across my chest with honor, respect and the privilege of being apart of something way greater then myself. You taught and showed me the true meaning of team work, family, fight and taking the jugular. I loved every moment and thanks to you, I bleed blue and gold!

Thank you, Reggie, for coming into my life and seeing my potential and doing all you have done to help me reach it. I have been so inspired and so enlightened by your words, ideas and experience that you continue to share. You are a true champion in life and your will to help others succeed is one I've never seen before. I am so grateful for you and love the power of your positivity, enthusiasm, and heart. Thank you for pushing me and challenging me and for including me with Mr. Norris and Professor David Dunn. I am humbled and love you all.

Cung, my true friend. You work harder than anyone I know and never stop. Thank you for including me and believing in me. I love you and love your wife Suzan as well. Thank you for having my back and for being there for me. You never cease to amaze me or disappoint. I am so appreciative for you and will always do what I can to help you on your journey as well. You are a real friend and a dedicated person to his family and work, it's refreshing to see. Thank you for being such a great example for my boys also, they adore you.

Lindsey K., I love, love, love you! You are the most thoughtful and strong woman. Thank you for always making me feel so loved. You are so silly!! When I look at our text string, it's non stop photos of us trying to one up the other with ugly and goofy pictures of ourselves. You are hilarious. When I think of you, I just think of how much I love you and how much I know I can trust and count on you. You don't really realize how inspiring you are to other women. You have been through so much and are so resilient and graceful. You truly blow my mind. I am better because I know you and because you are my friend. Thank you for all the special years of friendship you've shown me.

To the Malloy family, and Chris in particular, you were a pillar and an example for me. I will never forget the flowers that came for me on my UCLA graduation day. Thank you to you and your family for all the love and support they always showed me. I had such tremendous respect for you all. You are all such an example of what family should look like and operate. Thank you for always being such a healthy example of that for me and for helping me through some tough times in my life. Your parents are to this day some of the most beautiful people I have ever met. Mary, still the bravest and most amazing little girl I ever met.

Frank M., thank you for teaching me about myself, my potential in business and the power of independence. You taught me to strive for the best and never to settle. You taught me about heart, humility and kindness. You told me to fall in love with whom I chose rather than someone I needed to be with. I take pride in caring for myself and believe I can-- thanks to you. Thank you for the loyalty of friendship and for taking me to see Phantom of the Opera in New York while we were there working. You are one of the most intelligent people and interesting people I've ever met Frank. I never had anyone like you in my life and am so grateful that I did.

  I actually had help to edit this book from one of the most amazing, accomplished, women I have ever met. Shannon. She is a mother of four and possibly has the biggest heart of anyone I know. You are brilliant, intuitive, detailed, organized, brave, generous, and I know you fight hard for me to let you love me like you do. You have reminded me who I am more times than I'd like to admit. You see into the dark spaces of my mind and comfort me when I feel afraid to face the world. You know when I need a hug without even needing to see me and love my kids like they were your own. I always wonder what I did so great to deserve a woman like you to walk into my life, I truly will never know. You're a sink, ride or die friend that is always making sure I know how much I am loved by you and others. You can reach me like no one else can. I don't have words for how grateful I am for you in my life. Thank you for being a light in my life and for helping to get this book finished. Thank you for being part of True Boundaries and the Foundation, it wouldn't be as fun or the same without you. I love you, always always.

Courtenay, my best friend of 19 years. You are the longest and truest female friend I have ever had. You are not only beautiful on the outside but you're one of the strongest and most beautiful people on the inside. You have been a support to me in my worst times and been at my side during some of my best. Thank you for standing by me for so long, being a rock, dependable, loyal and strong for me all these years. I hope to share many more years of friendship with you. I am so proud of you Courtster for all you have become and accomplished. Thank you for literally holding my hand at times through this life. The way you have fought your battles outside as well as inside are inspiring. You are a warrior, brilliant and amazing in my eyes. I wouldn't be where I am today without you.

Damian, you're an angel in my life. You brought me into your home and off the streets and gave me family, brotherhood and lots of laughs. As far back as I can remember, you have been there. I am so proud of you with all you've accomplished. You are and will always be my brother and I love you so very much. My only complaint is that I never see enough of you.

Debby, you have been like a sister since we met. Thank you for being so supportive of me, for the love, laughter and for being there for me. Thank you for being such a great example of what a hard working mother should look like, never taking time from your boys and still making time for everyone and everything else. I love you so much!

Ray M., thank you for your loyalty, support, and for your friendship. You are very special to me and I am truly touched by all you have shared with me. You make me a better friend and person and I am grateful you came into my life. Keep being that guy who doesn't settle for less than he deserves and keep being the amazing single dad that you are. You are going big places, I am grateful to be on the sidelines to watch you go. You deserve the most love and the very best that this life has to offer. I wish you always lived with me, best roommate ever! Thank you for being the definition of a friend.

Sunny G., whom I've known since I was 14, thank you for pushing me to be the best surfer I could. Thank you for clearing whole line-ups so I could catch all the waves!

The boys and I love you tremendously. You are a champion inside and out. Your level of vulnerability you share with the world is amazing and you will alway hold such a special place in my heart. We have been through a ton together in both our lives. I am so happy to know you and to have been such a big part of all you are and all you've done and accomplished.

Thank you to my acting coaches, Steven Anderson and Tom Ardavany. Thank you for helping me to understand what it means to live in the moment and also the magic that comes in shaping our space and time. My journey in acting will hopefully resume one day when my boys are bigger. I sure love that craft. Thank you to both of you for always pushing me out of my comfort zone emotionally and mentally.

Joseph S, my most favorite Aussie! One of the best Dads on this planet and one of the most amazing humans I know. We go back 20 years plus and you have always believed in me, more at times than I believed in myself. I am so lucky to call you my friend, I am so proud of you and always in awe of your mind and drive. You are such a whole man in every sense of what a man should be. I love you dearly and am excited to watch you rise to top of everything you put your mind and energy into. Thank you for the years and years of true and honest friendship.

Harlan, I'm not sure I would have gotten back onto the mats without you. You literally picked me up, put my gi back on me and said, "You aren't allowed to quit!" You allowed me to be me and had my back through one of the hardest times in my life. You listened and were there for me and I am forever thankful to you for that. I pray for many more years of friendship with you. I love you dearly and am grateful for your presence in my life.

Johnny F, thank you for reaching out to me when I was down and for welcoming me into your Alliance family. I am grateful for the friendship that I share with you and to all the many people there who have helped my jiu-jitsu grow. You and Michella are family to me and I am forever grateful for your kindness and generosity.

Thank you Dodger God for being such a positive presence for me since I was 20 years old. I love you like my big brother. You're an amazing man and person. Thank you for trusting me with so many secrets and for always being there for me. If not for you, I wouldn't have met Mark and who knows if I would have kids or not by now. Godparent to my boys, I love you always.

Jean-yves, thank you for showing me how to really ride a horse and for bringing Kid Vicious into my life. Your love of horses is one we share. You are one of the best people I know and one of my most loyal and truest friends. Never a day without serious laughter with you. Thank you always JY.

Ryan R, Alicia, Leah, Satu, Julie, Lisa Lisa, Tarsis, Rickson G, Elias, Cozmo, Zoey, Aaron C, Anna, Cat Z, Keiser G, Jon S, David D, Flavio A, Lyle C, Todd A, Orlando S, Alfredo, Xande, Saulo, Mark B, Rillion G, Daniel D, Christopher D, Bomba, and Jay G…thank all of you for getting me back on the mats and keeping me here. My heart was broken and piece by piece it has been repaired by people like you who have supported and stood by me through a difficult time. Thank you for your kindness, friendship, and for believing in me on and off the mats.

Brian R, I owe Nick a thank you and my gratitude for bringing you into my life. You two are fucking badasses. No other way to say it. Thank you for having my back at hello. The first time I met you, I knew you would be in my life the rest of my life. You are all heart and wear a shield not many could penetrate. Thank you for sharing you with me and for inspiring me to take my business to another level. Thank you for your support and for being so protective of me. Your belief in me and kind words have picked me up more times then you know. Thank you for all you do for me, you make me better in every way.

Thank you Stig S for pushing me and believing in my ideas, my creativity and my abilities. Thank you for helping with my website and for encouraging me to keep going when I thought I couldn't go anymore. Your work, talents and abilities are awe inspiring, thank you for allowing me into your world and for inspiring me to go big in mine.

Demi L, thank you for the opportunity to work with you. You blow my mind every time we are together. Your attention to detail and your fierceness are what make you great in all you do. It is my pleasure and honor to be your professor in such a special art as jiu-jitsu. You melt my heart and motivate me to stay at the top of my own game. You are an amazing young woman with a beautiful and long life ahead of you. I look forward to being apart of it with you and being there when you get your black belt one day. Keep climbing your mountain and know that you will always have me near to lean on when you need to. God bless you woman, I love you.

Roger Y, Thank you my bruin brother for reminding me that it's never too late to catch our dreams. You are proof that we can come back even and come back around for the chance even a better version of ourselves than what we were before. I am blessed to have the people I have mentioned walk into my life and you are one of those extraordinary ones. I am truly so grateful for you and look forward to projects with you in the future. You my friend are an amazing human.

Thank you Steven Lyon for your long time friendship and for shooting the cover of this book for me. I am so proud of the work you are doing with the Rhino and wildlife in Africa. I believe in you and know that all the incredible projects you have going will come to fruition. Your heart and mind are in the right place. You are talented beyond measure and are beautiful inside and out. www.stevenlyon.com to see this man's work and to get involved with his Save the Rhino movement.

Thank you to all the little league boys who have played on my teams in the past, present and hopefully the future. I learn from all of you and it is such pure joy to watch you grow and learn the special game of baseball. There is no other game that parallels life like baseball and it's been my honor and privilege to coach you and to get to be a part of such an influential and special time in your lives. I will always remember Bruce Whittaker, my little league coach who inspired me and was always kind with me. He taught me the game and more importantly, he taught me to believe in myself. I love you Bruce and because of you, I try to do the same with every child that comes through my teams.

There are groups of people in Dana Point, at Salt Creek beach where I surfed everyday, Killer Dana surf shop for being my first sponsor in surfing, all the people in the surfing industry that believed in me. Thank you Cordell for always coming through with my boards and for being one of the most loving people and friends on the planet. You are rare, unique and someone I brag about all the time. John W., you are the bomb. Thank you for helping to get my modeling career going back when I was 17. You are family to me and someone I have deep respect and love for. Thank you for being a constant in my life, I love you Watty. Greg Arnet for giving me a quiet, awe inspiring place to finish my book and retreat to when I needed to ground my feet to the earth. Thank you for sponsoring me and for believing in me as well. Your ranch is one of my most favorite places on earth. Thank you Greg for being there for me since I was 15. For staying in touch all these years. Great friends and loved ones are hard to come by. You are family to me and there isn't anything I wouldn't do for you. I love you and always will. Thank you Paul & Stephanie Gomez for your support and for being such amazing role models. I have always looked up to you both and admired the love you have for one another. Anthony G, I am so proud of you and the empire that you've built, you continue to blow my mind and I am so grateful to have you in my life after all these years. Dave C, Richie H, Kenny, The Boehne's, you all touched and influenced my life for the best.

Thank you to all the extraordinary people who have touched my life and helped me to become who I am today. Thank you to the people I didn't mention as well and the ones I've loved and lost. Every human needs support, love, affection, friends, interaction and relationships to truly grow. We weren't put on this earth for less than that. Nothing is more important than the relationships we cultivate and the ones we love. Life is fragile and time waits for no one. Be bold when it comes to love and sharing what you have to offer. Your friends and especially your loved ones deserve the best version of you.

To contact the author:

www.trueboundaries.com

www.trueboundariescharitablefoundation.com

Danielle Martin on Facebook

True Boundaries Charitable Foundation on Facebook

Instagram: @trueboundaries & @officaldaniellemartin

Twitter: @hellodmartin

A part of the proceeds from this book will go to The True Boundaries Foundation as well as other charities with whom we partner with.

The True Boundaries Charitable Organization brings awareness to assault, the largest most under reported crime in our country. It brings awareness to domestic violence and takes a solid stand against bullying.

Made in the USA
Las Vegas, NV
28 April 2022